U.S. Border Control

by Crystal D. McCage

Current Issues

ReferencePoint
Press™

San Diego, CA

© 2009 ReferencePoint Press, Inc.

For more information, contact:
ReferencePoint Press, Inc.
PO Box 27779
San Diego, CA 92198
www.ReferencePointPress.com

Picture credits:
Maury Aaseng: 65
AP Images: 11, 15
Tony Strom: 30–33, 46–49, 63–67, 81–83

LIBRARY OF CONGRESS CATALOGING-IN-PUBLICATION DATA

McCage, Crystal D.
   U.S. border control / by Crystal D. McCage.
      p. cm. — (Compact research series)
   Includes bibliographical references and index.
   ISBN-13: 978-1-60152-052-4 (hardback)
   ISBN-10: 1-60152-052-2 (hardback)
   1. Border security—United States. 2. Border patrols—United States. 3. Border security—Canada. 4. Border security—Mexico. I. Title.
   JV6483.M335 2009
   363.28'50973—dc22
                                                                          2007048332

Contents

Foreword

❝ Where is the knowledge we have lost in information? ❞

—"The Rock," T.S. Eliot.

As modern civilization continues to evolve, its ability to create, store, distribute, and access information expands exponentially. The explosion of information from all media continues to increase at a phenomenal rate. By 2020 some experts predict the worldwide information base will double every 73 days. While access to diverse sources of information and perspectives is paramount to any democratic society, information alone cannot help people gain knowledge and understanding. Information must be organized and presented clearly and succinctly in order to be understood. The challenge in the digital age becomes not the creation of information, but how best to sort, organize, enhance, and present information.

ReferencePoint Press developed the *Compact Research* series with this challenge of the information age in mind. More than any other subject area today, researching current issues can yield vast, diverse, and unqualified information that can be intimidating and overwhelming for even the most advanced and motivated researcher. The *Compact Research* series offers a compact, relevant, intelligent, and conveniently organized collection of information covering a variety of current topics ranging from illegal immigration and methamphetamine to diseases such as anorexia and meningitis.

The series focuses on three types of information: objective single-author narratives, opinion-based primary source quotations, and facts and statistics. The clearly written objective narratives provide context and reliable background information. Primary source quotes are carefully selected and cited, exposing the reader to differing points of view. And facts and statistics sections aid the reader in evaluating perspectives. Presenting these key types of information creates a richer, more balanced learning experience.

For better understanding and convenience, the series enhances information by organizing it into narrower topics and adding design features that make it easy for a reader to identify desired content. For example, in *Compact Research: Illegal Immigration*, a chapter covering the economic impact of illegal immigration has an objective narrative explaining the various ways the economy is impacted, a balanced section of numerous primary source quotes on the topic, followed by facts and full-color illustrations to encourage evaluation of contrasting perspectives.

The ancient Roman philosopher Lucius Annaeus Seneca wrote, "It is quality rather than quantity that matters." More than just a collection of content, the *Compact Research* series is simply committed to creating, finding, organizing, and presenting the most relevant and appropriate amount of information on a current topic in a user-friendly style that invites, intrigues, and fosters understanding.

U.S. Border Control at a Glance

U.S. Borders

The U.S. border with Mexico is over 1,952 miles (3,141km) long. The U.S. border with Canada is the longest border in the world at 5,522 miles (8,887km).

U.S. Border Patrol

Over 11,000 Border Patrol officers work along the U.S.-Mexican border. Only about 1,000 officers patrol the U.S.-Canadian border.

Illegal Immigration

An estimated 1 million people cross illegally into the United States each year. About 66 percent of these people are Mexican.

Homeland Security

Since the attacks on the United States on September 11, 2001, U.S. officials and citizens are concerned that would-be terrorists could enter the United States illegally among the more than one million who enter without proper documentation each year.

Federal Spending

In 2007 the U.S. federal budget for U.S. Customs and Border Protection was $7.84 billion.

U.S. Economy

Experts disagree about the costs and benefits of illegal immigrants to the U.S. economy. Some argue that illegal immigrants perform jobs that

Americans would be unwilling to do. Others contend that Americans would be willing to perform these jobs and that illegal immigrants drive down wages.

Government and Politics

The U.S. government has struggled in recent years to improve public perception of its border control policies. Poll results show that many Americans do not feel secure with the current state of border control.

Border Control Solutions

Solutions to border control problems vary widely. Some argue for more and better fences, while others argue that border security will remain a problem as long as economic differences between the United States and Mexico remain so strong. Polls show Americans are largely divided when it comes to the best way to control U.S. borders.

Overview

Overview

66America is suffering for the lack of comprehensive border and immigration policies. Many current U.S. laws regarding immigration and border policy are either outmoded or ineffective, and go unenforced.99

—U.S. Border Control, "Our Mission."

66 The men and women of our Border Patrol are doing a fine job in difficult circumstances, and over the past five years, they have apprehended and sent home about six million people entering America illegally.99

—George W. Bush, "The President's Strategy for Accelerating Border Security."

Border control for any country means controlling immigration, controlling the movement of its citizens, preventing the smuggling of illegal items such as drugs and weapons, and even controlling the spread of human and animal disease.

Defending U.S. Borders

In the United States two land borders must be controlled—the border with Mexico and the border with Canada. The U.S.-Mexican border consists of 1,952 miles (3,141km) of terrain, and according to U.S. Customs and Border Protection, the border itself is often difficult to discern as it runs through deserts, canyons, and across mountains. The U.S.-Canadian border is the longest common border in the world at 5,522 miles (8,887km) long, including 1,539 miles (2,477km) between Alaska and Canada.

The 2 borders have a significantly different number of security personnel present. According to the U.S. Department of Homeland Security, an estimated 1,000 border security personnel patrol the U.S. and Canadian border, compared to an estimated 11,000 to 12,000 who patrol the U.S. and Mexican border.

In addition to some of the longest land borders in the world, the U.S. Border Patrol must control over 2,000 miles (3,219km) of the busy coastal waters surrounding the Florida coasts and the coast of Southern California, areas where illegal entry into the United States is of particular concern. The U.S. Border Patrol must also monitor, in cooperation with the U.S. Coast Guard, a total of 95,000 miles (152,888km) of maritime border.

U.S. Border Patrol

The U.S. Border Patrol has existed in various forms since the late nineteenth century. It was started in response to the Chinese Exclusion Act of 1882, which suspended the immigration of Chinese people to the United States. When Chinese immigrants began trying to enter the United States via Mexico, groups organized to patrol the southwestern border of the United States. In March 1915 the U.S. Congress authorized a group of Mounted Guards who had been working to patrol U.S. borders in California. It did not take long for the federal government to understand the importance of border patrol, and in May 1924 the U.S. Border Patrol was founded as an agency of the U.S. Department of Labor. Today the U.S. Border Patrol is an agency of the U.S. Department of Homeland Security. The U.S. Border Patrol employs more than 13,000, and that number is expected to rise to nearly 20,000 by 2009.

> **In the United States two land borders must be controlled— the border with Mexico and the border with Canada.**

In the early 1990s the U.S. Border Patrol changed strategies from a focus on apprehension of illegal immigrants to the prevention of illegal immigration. Fences and walls equipped with cameras were built along high traffic areas for illegal immigration along parts of the southern borders of California and Texas. While this infrastructure significantly reduced the number of illegal border crossings in these areas, the Border Patrol found that activity increased elsewhere, such as along Arizona's southern border. Since September 11, 2001, border control issues have become even more significant. Now, not only are many Americans concerned about illegal immigrants having a negative impact on the nation's economy, they are concerned about illegal immigrants who might be members of terrorist organizations.

Illegal Immigration and Border Control

Many Americans who are concerned about U.S. border control do not feel the U.S. government does a good job with the responsibility, especially when it comes to illegal immigration. In a 2006 poll conducted by Public Agenda, about three-quarters of Americans who were surveyed said that they were worried "it's too easy for illegal immigrants to enter the U.S." According to the same poll, three-quarters of Americans said they would give the U.S. government a "'C' or worse for protecting U.S. borders from illegal immigration."[1] Indeed, in 2005 government estimates indicated that about 11 million illegal immigrants reside inside U.S. borders, and that number has continued to rise.

> **Indeed, in 2005 government estimates indicated that about 11 million illegal immigrants reside inside U.S. borders, and that number has continued to rise.**

What Brings Illegal Immigrants to the United States?

Many attribute the increasing number of illegal immigrants in the United States to strong motivations for people to enter the United States. Most economists point to the economic differences between the United States and Mexico. The United States is the only developed nation to share a land border with a developing nation. This certainly presents problems when it comes to border control. When a poor Mexican citizen can make

U.S. Border Patrol agents patrol the U.S.-Mexico border. Over 11,000 Border Patrol officers work along the U.S.-Mexican border. Only about 1,000 officers patrol the U.S.-Canadian border.

more in one hour than he or she can in a whole day in Mexico, it does not take an economist to recognize a clear motivation to cross the border.

Most illegal immigrants are motivated by economic opportunities, and in recent decades, life for poor Mexicans has become even more difficult. Many poor Mexican farmers are without jobs and feel their only hope is to try to make a living in the United States. The Mexican government has failed to improve the standard of living in Mexico. According to a recent report from the World Bank, corruption in the Mexican government and economy is extreme and they must be reformed significantly before any real economic changes can take place.

Economic Concerns

Certainly, the economic cost of weak U.S. border control is one of the most controversial discussions related to this issue. Many point out that illegal immigrants are willing to take jobs that most Americans will not take. Still others argue that the only people benefiting from illegal alien workers are the companies who employ illegal immigrants "off-the-books" for low wages and no benefits. The reality of the situation is complicated, and the truth depends upon whom you ask. The American perception that illegal immigrants are taking jobs and driving down wages is supported by some research. According to George Borjas, a professor at Harvard University and an immigration expert, heavy immigration since 1980 decreased the wages of American-born men without a high school education by 7.4 percent. Borjas also found that immigration is particularly a hardship for minority, American-born men in the United States because they are more likely to compete with illegal immigrants for jobs.

Of course, research also supports the economic benefits to America of illegal immigrant workers. A recent study by the Udall Center for Studies in Public Policy at the University of Arizona found that illegal immigrants are not "stealing" American jobs, because they are most likely to perform low-paying jobs in agriculture and the service industry that many Americans would not take. The study also found that illegal immigrants were contributing more to the economy than they were taking. The study reported: "Non-citizens, for their part, contributed $28.9 billion, or 8 percent of Arizona's economic output, resulting in 278,000 full-time equivalent jobs. Their output included $10 billion in labor income, and $3.3 billion in other property income. The state tax revenues resulting from this economic activity were approximately $1.08 billion."[2]

What Is Being Done to Protect U.S. Borders?

And while the economic impact of illegal immigration is at the forefront of the discussion of border control at this time, security is another important issue. Crimes committed by illegal immigrants, especially in border communities, are a big concern for many Americans. Although federal laws make tracking criminal activity by illegal aliens difficult, the U.S. Government Accountability Office (GAO) has conducted some research into the criminal activity of some illegal aliens. The GAO is an independent, nonpartisan agency that works for Congress. It is sometimes referred to as the "congressional watchdog" because it investigates how the federal government spends taxpayer dollars. While the GAO provides no statistics on the number of illegal aliens in federal prisons, it did report that in 2003,

74,000 illegal aliens remained in state prisons and 147,000 illegal aliens were imprisoned in local jails. In one study, the GAO examined the arrest history of 55,332 illegal aliens and found that they were arrested a total of 459,614 times, for an average of 8 arrests per illegal alien. Moreover, Heather Mac Donald, senior fellow at the Manhattan Institute for Policy Research, testified before the House Judiciary Subcommittee on Immigration, Border Security, and Claims that "in Los Angeles, 95 percent of all outstanding warrants for homicide in the first half of 2004 (which totaled 1,200 to 1,500) targeted illegal aliens."[3]

Of course, it is important to note that not all illegal immigrants are criminals. In fact, illegal immigrants are often victims of crime but are afraid to report it out of fear of being deported. However, experts like Mac Donald point out that current laws protecting illegal immigrants make it difficult for law enforcement officials to stop the illegal aliens who do commit crimes.

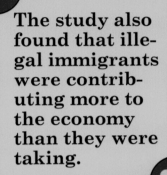

The study also found that illegal immigrants were contributing more to the economy than they were taking.

Terrorism is another security concern for the U.S. Border Patrol. The porous borders in the United States would make it easy for would-be terrorists to cross into the country. According to U.S. admiral James Loy, deputy secretary of the Department of Homeland Security:

> Recent information from ongoing investigations, detentions, and emerging threat streams strongly suggests that al Qaeda has considered using the southwest border to infiltrate the United States. Several al Qaeda leaders believe operatives can pay their way into the country through Mexico and also believe illegal entry is more advantageous than legal entry for operational security reasons.[4]

In his book *Illegals: The Imminent Threat Posed by Our Unsecured U.S.-Mexico Border*, investigative journalist Jon E. Dougherty points to a specific example that has raised concerns:

> There are also concerns that some illegals may be coming here specifically to commit terrorist acts against Americans,

some on the scale of the 9-11 attacks. One case that caused such concern involved a Mexican alien in Virginia who was arrested after police received a tip he was planning to poison water supplies in the winter of 2002. Virginia authorities, in conjunction with the FBI, began an investigation of Ipolito "Polo" Campos, who was living illegally near Virginia's eastern shore despite being expelled from the United States once before. According to court records, Campos had told an associate, who later informed the authorities, that he was from an "Arabian" country and "if he did not poison the water someone would kill him."[5]

Due to elevated concerns about illegal immigration into the United States, the federal government has worked to increase the funding and staffing for border security significantly in the last decade. In the 2007 federal budget, President George W. Bush requested an additional $702 million for U.S. Customs and Border Protection, bringing the total requested for 2007 to $7.8 billion. This 2007 budget provided for 1,500 additional U.S. Border Patrol agents at a cost of $458.9 million, $50.8 million for the construction of permanent vehicle barriers along the Arizona border, and an increase in Weapons of Mass Destruction Detection staffing in U.S. ports at a cost of $12 million. These are just a few examples of the kinds of programs the U.S. government must fund to maintain and improve border security. The White House reports positive results from its recent efforts to better address border security issues. The concern for many American citizens is the fact that the U.S. government estimates that for every one illegal immigrant who is caught at the border, about three illegal immigrants make it across.

> " Due to elevated concerns about illegal immigration into the United States, the federal government has worked to increase the funding and staffing for border security significantly in the last decade. "

Out of frustration over perceived weaknesses in U.S. border control, some Americans who live in border areas have developed different kinds of volunteer border patrols. The most well known of the volunteer border security organizations is the Minuteman Project. Hundreds of volunteers in the Minuteman Project began watching the border in April 2005.

Volunteer Border Security

Out of frustration over perceived weaknesses in U.S. border control, some Americans who live in border areas have developed different kinds of volunteer border patrols. The most famous of the volunteer border security organizations is the Minuteman Project. Hundreds of volunteers in the Minuteman Project began watching the border and assisting Border Patrol agents in April 2005. Focused mainly along the border between Arizona and Mexico, Minutemen are often armed with handguns but are supposed to simply report illegal crossing to the authorities. Although Minuteman Project leaders claim that Border Patrol agents are appreciative of their efforts, the U.S. Border Patrol has issued official statements that these volunteer groups, though they are doing nothing illegal by monitoring the border, could end up in violent situations.

The effectiveness of the Minuteman Project is debatable, but the controversy stirred by the organization cannot be debated. While President George W. Bush has called members of the group vigilantes, other government officials have praised the Minutemen. California governor Arnold Schwarzenegger has complimented the volunteers for their efforts to help secure the nation's borders. Still, reports of racism and the potential for violence plague the organization. While the group's founder, Jim Gilchrist, says that the organization is multiethnic and that racism will not be tolerated within the organization, individual members of the organization have made racial slurs about immigrants to the media. Whatever the case, the Minuteman Project has certainly gained a lot of media attention, and state branches of the group have popped up all over the United States.

What Is the Future of U.S. Border Control?

While such issues remain so controversial, it is difficult for government officials to agree upon and assess what would work best when it comes to the future of U.S. Border Control. Those who point to the economic benefits of illegal immigrants call for such things as amnesty programs or, at the very least, making it easier for these workers to be employed in the United States. President George W. Bush's immigration reform policy called for a stronger temporary worker program. According to Bush, "new immigration laws should serve the economic needs of our country. If an American employer is offering a job that American citizens are not willing to take, we ought to welcome into our country a person who will fill that job."[6] Of course, critics of Bush's proposal point out that the main people who benefit from temporary worker programs are big businesses who get away with paying people low wages. They say that Americans lose jobs and wages are lowered, and at the same time, the immigrants end up working for years without a fair path to citizenship.

There are also some who propose building better physical barriers along the borders. In 2006 the federal government approved building an additional 700 miles (1,127km) of border fence sections in key crossing areas in California, Arizona, New Mexico, and Texas. While funding for such fences has proved problematic for the U.S. government and their effectiveness has been questioned, many government officials, especially representatives from border states, continue to call for more fences. Arizona representative J.D. Hayworth has supported fence proposals. Organizations such as the Minuteman Border Fence support fences and walls that might at least minimize border crossings and have even begun building fences with donated funds and materials.

Economists continue to argue that the only way to cut down on the high amount of illegal immigration and thus make it easier to secure the borders is to work to address the economic motivations that are so strong as to motivate people to risk their lives to enter the United States illegally. Many Americans want the federal government to enforce laws making it illegal to hire undocumented workers. To alleviate this problem, Americans are even willing to provide more opportunities for temporary workers in the United States. In fact, a 2007 poll conducted by the Vernon K. Krieble Foundation indicates that most Americans understand that border boundaries and more border agents will not solve border security issues by themselves and that the United States needs a better system for handling temporary workers.

> " In 2006 the federal government approved building an additional 700 miles (1,127km) of border fence sections in key crossing areas in California, Arizona, New Mexico, and Texas. "

Clearly, U.S. border control is a controversial issue with many sides. The future of border control is complicated by disagreement among government leaders and among American citizens who struggle with this issue in their daily lives.

What Are the Impediments to Effective Border Control?

66We must have secure borders and strong border control. We must return illegal aliens to their homes, especially criminal aliens.99

—Al Gore, Town Hall Meeting.

66I'm never going back to El Salvador. I'm still safer and better off cleaning a home here than I would be working at a factory in El Salvador. I'll hide if I have to, but this is where I want to live.99

—Leticia, U.S. immigrant with temporary status.

Because the United States consists of large and diverse borders, effective border control is difficult and costly. The United States has two land borders that must be controlled: the Mexican border and the Canadian border. The U.S.-Mexican border consists of 1,952 miles (3,141km) of terrain, and according to U.S. Customs and Border Protection, "often, the border is a barely discernible line in uninhabited deserts, canyons, or mountains."[7] Historically, the greatest security of this border has been near urban areas such as San Diego, California, and El Paso, Texas. These areas have had the highest numbers of illegal border crossings in the past. Recently, however, as border security has been strengthened in and around these urban areas, an increasing number of people are trying to cross illegally into the United States from Mexico through barren deserts and over perilous mountains, areas that are difficult for the U.S. Border Patrol to control.

The U.S.-Canadian border is the longest common border in the world and is 5,522 miles (8,887km) long, including 1,539 miles (2,477km) between Alaska and Canada. This border is sometimes referred to as the world's "longest undefended border." However, it is actually controlled and monitored, just not nearly as heavily as the U.S.-Mexican border. Although border control of the U.S.-Canadian border was increased after the terrorist attacks on September 11, 2001, security along this border remains relatively low, with an estimated 1,000 border security personnel between the United States and Canada compared to an estimated 11,000 to 12,000 between the United States and Mexico.

Border control in the United States is not limited to land borders, however. The U.S. Border Patrol must closely monitor over 2,000 miles (3,219km) of the highly-trafficked coastal waters surrounding Florida and Southern California. And in partnership with the U.S. Coast Guard the U.S. Border Patrol is responsible for a total of 95,000 miles (152,888km) of maritime border.

Creation of the U.S. Border Patrol

With borders this extensive, the United States attempts to control its borders for a variety of reasons, but most often for immigration. Between 1848 and 1882, about 300,000 Chinese immigrants entered the United States. Although many came in search of gold in California, many ended up as laborers. The Chinese were considered "unassimilable," or unable or unwilling to assimilate to American culture. When Chinese immigrants sought to enter the United States along the U.S.-Mexican border, groups that would be the beginnings of the U.S. Border Patrol were formed.

> " The U.S. Border Patrol must closely monitor over 2,000 miles (3,219km) of the highly-trafficked coastal waters surrounding Florida and Southern California. "

The U.S. Border Patrol Today

Today the U.S. Border Patrol employs more than 13,000 agents and must patrol over 19,000 miles (30,578km) of land and sea borders. In the early 1990s the U.S. Border Patrol changed strategies from a focus on apprehension of illegal immigrants to the prevention of illegal immigration. Fences and walls equipped with cameras were built along high traffic areas for illegal immigration across parts of the southern borders of California and Texas. While this infrastructure significantly reduced the number of illegal border crossings in these areas, the Border Patrol found that activity increased elsewhere, such as along the Arizona border.

Since September 11, 2001, border control issues have become even more important. Now, not only are many Americans concerned about illegal immigrants having a negative impact on the nation's economy, they are concerned about illegal immigrants who might be members of terrorist organizations. After September 11, 2001, the U.S. Border Patrol became a part of the Department of Homeland Security under the agency of Customs and Border Protection. Although the U.S. Border Patrol was expanded significantly with plans to nearly double the number of agents, border control remains one of the most controversial and divisive issues in the United States today.

> **Although the U.S. Border Patrol was expanded significantly with plans to nearly double the number of agents, border control remains one of the most controversial and divisive issues in the United States today.**

Illegal Immigration and U.S. Border Control

One of the most important issues related to U.S. border security is whether border control policies are effective in controlling illegal immigration into the United States. While the U.S. government continues to make efforts in this area, illegal immigration is on the rise. In 1986 Congress passed the Immigration Reform and Control Act. This act, signed into law by President Ronald Reagan, granted amnesty to an estimated 2.7 million illegal immigrants and made it illegal for companies to hire any immigrants who did not possess lawful work authorization. At the time, this law was seen as the solution to a growing illegal immigration problem during the 1980s. However, while 2.7 million illegal immigrants were granted amnesty, the part of the law requiring employers to hire only workers with proper documentation included many exceptions, and the law has been difficult to enforce.

While the estimated number of illegal immigrants inside America's borders decreased after the 1986 Immigration Reform and Control Act, it did not take long for these numbers to increase dramatically. Estimates have grown from around 2.5 million in 1989 to over 11 million in 2005, and estimates for the number of illegal immigrants living in the United States today range from a conservative 12 million to a high of 20 million, with the majority of these illegal immigrants being from Mexico, evidence that the 1986 legislation has not accomplished its goals. Certainly, illegal immigration is the biggest impediment to effective border control policy in the United States.

When it comes to illegal immigration across the U.S.-Mexican border, the Mexican economy is a significant push for many people.

Push Factors for Illegal Immigration

Any time people immigrate to another country, either legally or illegally, usually several factors play a role in their decision to move. The push factors are the issues that "push" people out of their home countries, making it important for them to leave. When it comes to illegal immigration across the U.S.-Mexican border, the Mexican economy is a significant push for many people. According to a 2000 estimate from the U.S. Immigration and Naturalization Service, well over two-thirds of the illegal immigrants in the United States are from Mexico. The fact is that the United States has one of the strongest economies in the world, while Mexico's economy is much weaker. The United States, the richest country in the world, shares a significant land border with a developing nation. Mexican people thus have a great incentive to want to immigrate to the United States, even if they have to do so illegally.

In Mexico, social stratification is a significant problem. In 2000, 60 percent of the population was poor, and in that same year, 40 percent of the income earned in Mexico was earned by only 10 percent of the population. Moreover, many Mexican states have a housing shortage, and lower-class Mexican families live in single-room structures and have few public services. While education is required for all Mexican children up to the ninth grade, the opportunities for education are small for poorer Mexicans, making it almost impossible for a poor Mexican family to rise out of poverty. In May 2007 the World Bank reported key problems in the Mexican economy, citing issues such as monopolies, corruption, and poor education.

"Pull" Factors for Illegal Immigration

Just as the poor Mexican economy pushes Mexicans out of their home country, the lure of better jobs in a strong economy "pulls" many Mexicans toward the United States. A reality of the strong U.S. economy is that it is built upon a base of illegal immigrant workers who supply companies with cheap labor and perform jobs some say American citizens are unwilling to perform. The 1986 Immigration Reform and Control Act made it illegal for United States companies to hire illegal immigrants who lack proper documentation to work in the United States. However, illegal immigrants still find work. According to John Gay, who is a Washington lobbyist for the hotel and lodging industry, American citizens are unwilling to clean hotel rooms or change bed pans in nursing homes. In fact, according to *USA Today* reporter Laura Parker: "Jobs in poultry plants across the South, once held almost exclusively by American blacks, are now dominated by Mexican immigrants. Textile plants run largely on the labors of Hispanic workers. In the Kentucky coal fields, mining companies are considering recruiting miners from the Ukraine."[8]

These jobs are alluring to people who may make only a minimum wage in Mexico of 52.59 pesos, or about $4.85, per day. When people can make more than that in a single hour of work in the United States, it is easy to see why border control between the United States and Mexico can be difficult. The allure is so strong that many illegal immigrants are willing to risk their lives to get inside the U.S. border. According to Richard Rodriguez, an award-winning Mexican American author: "You have Mexicans who look at the United States and see this line of border patrolmen. They know that that's what the law is but they also know that beyond the law, there's somebody that will hire them at a drycleaners."[9]

As the United States has increased border security, crossing the U.S.-Mexican border has become even more difficult and much more dangerous, but people are still willing to take the chance. The economic benefits make it worth it. According to Border Patrol agents, the number of illegal immigrants caught in dangerous border crossings increased significantly at the turn of the millennium. People are regularly caught hiding in trunks, gas tanks, and even under truck hoods near engines, and the people who are caught are frequently the lucky ones. Many people die each year attempting dangerous border crossings, but most experts agree it is difficult to deter illegal immigrants who are willing to risk their lives. According to a 2001 CNN report, one illegal Mexican immigrant living in California reported that he was able to make a dangerous journey over the mountains but that his pregnant wife was unable to make the arduous journey. Since then, his pregnant wife has attempted to cross the border twice, once inside a car trunk. According to the man, "She needs to be here, you know. And we risk our lives in order to get her a better life . . . to be living in Mexico it's worse than to risk your life."[10]

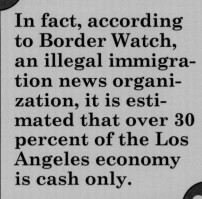

In fact, according to Border Watch, an illegal immigration news organization, it is estimated that over 30 percent of the Los Angeles economy is cash only.

Part of the problem is that U.S. companies have an incentive of sorts to hire illegal immigrant workers. Employers do not have to pay living wages or employment taxes for illegal workers, and a cash-only economy based on illegal workers has been built. Employers pay illegal workers cash and avoid taxes. The illegal workers who are paid cash avoid taxes. And the landlords who are paid in cash from the illegal workers avoid taxes. It is a vicious cycle but one that is a large part of the U.S. economy. In fact, according to Border Watch, an illegal immigration news organization, it is estimated that over 30 percent of the Los Angeles economy is cash only.

Researchers point out that the holes in the 1986 Immigration Reform and Control Act add to the lure of jobs for illegal immigrants by making it too easy for employers to hire illegal workers. In reality, the act is so flawed that even the employers who want to follow the law have difficulty.

According to a 2006 report from the *Christian Science Monitor*, when the 1986 act was passed, Congress did not want to establish a national identity card due to privacy concerns. Therefore, under the act, potential employees are able to present many forms of identification for employment. There are at least 25 different forms of identification potential employees can present to employers proving their eligibility to work in the United States. With the lack of consistency comes a lack in standards, and even the most earnest employers can have a hard time detecting fake documents. There are also no fines for employers as long as they are filling out the proper paperwork. Therefore, as long as they required a few of the 25 different documents and completed the required I-9 forms, they cannot be punished. According to Louis DeSepiro, professor of Latino studies at the University of California, this flawed system provides added incentives for illegal immigrants: "I don't think employer enforcement alone will stop illegal immigration. But it will decrease the incentive for a new migrant who doesn't have family here. That person wouldn't take the risk if he/she didn't have the confidence that he/she could move directly into a job."[11]

It seems certain that as long as there are jobs in the United States for illegal immigrants, border control will be complicated and costly.

What Are the Impediments to Effective Border Control?

66 Illegal immigration puts pressure on public schools and hospitals, it strains state and local budgets, and brings crime to our communities. These are real problems. Yet we must remember that the vast majority of illegal immigrants are decent people who work hard, support their families, practice their faith, and lead responsible lives. 99

—George W. Bush, "President Bush Addresses the Nation on Immigration Reform," The White House, May 15, 2006. www.whitehouse.gov.

Bush is the forty-third president of the United States, inaugurated in 2001.

66 It's wrong to condone illegal immigration that flouts our laws, strains our tolerance, taxes our resources. Even a nation of immigrants must have rules and conditions and limits. 99

—Former president Bill Clinton, "Commencement Address at Portland State University," June 13, 1998.

Clinton was the forty-second president of the United States and served from 1993 to 2001.

Bracketed quotes indicate conflicting positions.

* Editor's Note: While the definition of a primary source can be narrowly or broadly defined, for the purposes of Compact Research, a primary source consists of: 1) results of original research presented by an organization or researcher; 2) eyewitness accounts of events, personal experience, or work experience; 3) first-person editorials offering pundits' opinions; 4) government officials presenting political plans and/or policies; 5) representatives of organizations presenting testimony or policy.

> **"Cheap immigrant labor displaces American workers and cheats the taxpaying public in a variety of ways."**

—Don Huddle, in Charles P. Alexander, "A Most Debated Issue," *Time*, July 8, 1985. www.time.com.

Huddle is a professor of economics at Rice University.

> **"Unemployment has shrunk while the number of immigrants has grown. Guess they're not taking away American jobs."**

—American Immigration Law Foundation, immigration reform poster, www.ailf.org.

The American Immigration Law Foundation is an organization dedicated to increasing public understanding of immigration law and the value of immigrants to American culture.

> **"Immigration reform is a very multi-dimensional problem. For example, we must secure the border, but we must also have an employee verification system so that employers are not hiring anyone illegally. In order to have an employee verification system, we have to register the workers. In order to register the workers, we have to have them come out of the shadows. The whole thing ties together."**

—Carlos Gutierrez, "Ask the White House," The White House, June 25, 2007. www.whitehouse.gov.

Gutierrez is the thirty-fifth secretary of the U.S. Department of Commerce, the voice of business in government. He is the former chair of the board and chief executive officer of Kellogg Company and is currently a member of President George W. Bush's economic team.

66 Any reform of our immigration policies must begin first at the front line of the crisis: our border with Mexico. 99

—Lou Dobbs, "U.S. Policy on Immigration Is a Tragic Joke," *Arizona Republic*, November 3, 2007. www.azcentral.com.

Dobbs is the anchor and managing editor of the CNN news program *Lou Dobbs Tonight*.

66 We cannot get control of our borders until we do something about . . . a man or woman who is making fifty cents an hour in Mexico and can make ten bucks an hour in the United States, for a job that Americans will not do. 99

—Karl Rove, "On Immigration: Excerpts from the Aspen Ideas Festival," *Atlantic Monthly*, October 2006.

Rove was deputy chief of staff to President George W. Bush until his resignation in August 2007. Before working for Bush at the White House, Rove was a political consultant for Republican candidates.

66 I thought then [1986] that taking care of three million people illegally in the country would solve the problem once and for all. I found out, however, if you reward illegality, you get more of it. Today, as everybody has generally agreed, we have 12 million people here illegally. 99

—Charles Grassley, *New York Times*, June 12, 2007.

Grassley is a Republican senator from Iowa who has served as a member of the Senate since 1980.

66 Americans are in a show-me mood when it comes to immigration, and are oh-so aware that past border toughening and the 1986 amnesty for illegals did little to stem the flow. 99

—Editorial, *Christian Science Monitor*, November 29, 2005. www.csmonitor.com.

The *Christian Science Monitor* is an international newspaper started in 1908. The newspaper focuses on international and U.S. news.

---

66 Now 12 to 20 million illegal aliens who for 25 years have simply walked across, swam across, or were driven under cover of darkness across our nation's border feel they have endured the same comparable experience to the countless harrowing 'Underground Railroad' trips made by Harriett Tubman or Sojourner Truth through slave states to convey slaves freedom. Of course there is no logical comparison. 99

—Kevin Fobbbs, "Blacks Are Harmed By Illegal Immigration," The Conservative Brotherhood, July 24, 2006.

Fobbs is a conservative commentator, author, and political advisor from Michigan. He is a member of Michigan Republican State Committee and President of the National Urban Policy Action Council, a political organization promoting compassionate conservatism.

---

66 The American people get it, and they do have common sense and wisdom on this issue. They know repeating the fundamental mistakes of the 1986 bill, joining a big amnesty with inadequate enforcement, will cause the problem to grow and not diminish. They know promising enforcement after 30 years of broken promises isn't good enough. They know the so-called trigger is a joke because if the trigger is never pulled, the Z visas, the amnesty happens forever. 99

—Harry Reid, *Congressional Record*, U.S. Senate floor.

Reid is a Democratic senator from Nevada who has served in the Senate since 1982.

Facts and Illustrations

What Are the Impediments to Effective Border Control?

- America is the only **developed nation** in the world to share a large land border with a third-world nation, Mexico.

- Estimates about the number of illegal immigrants vary widely from **11 million** to **20 million**.

- About **60 percent** of the illegal immigrants in America have been here at least five years.

- Many illegal immigrants have had children in the United States, making those children **U.S. citizens**.

- Between **400,000** and **700,000** illegal immigrants enter the United States each year.

- According to a recent poll, **58 percent** of Mexicans said they believe the southwestern United States rightfully belonged to Mexico.

- Nearly **25 percent** of illegal immigrants live in California. Texas has the second-most undocumented immigrants at **14 percent**.

- Undocumented workers make up at least **12 percent** of the state of Arizona's workforce.

The Majority of Illegals Arrived After 1995

According to a 2006 study by the Pew Hispanic Center, most illegal immigrants to the United States are recent arrivals, with only 16 percent having been in the United States since the 1980s.

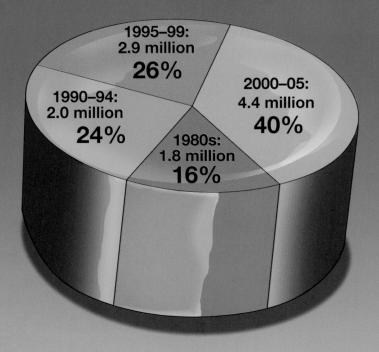

1995–99:
2.9 million
26%

1990–94:
2.0 million
24%

2000–05:
4.4 million
40%

1980s:
1.8 million
16%

Source: Jeffrey S. Passel, "The Size and Characteristics of the Unauthorized Migrant Population in the US," Pew Hispanic Center, March 2006. http://pewhispanic.org.

- According to a 2006 *Time* magazine poll, **89 percent** of Americans think illegal immigration into the United States is a problem.

- According to a study from the University of California, every day in the United States, workers gather in about **500 U.S. parking lots** and main streets hoping to be picked for construction or other jobs by drive-up employers. Three-quarters of these workers are illegal immigrants.

- Since 2000, births have been responsible for the **largest growth** with America's Latino population, not immigration.

- According to a *Washington Post* report, deporting the estimated **12 million** illegal immigrants who now live in the United States would require a caravan of **200,000** buses filled with people stretching from San Diego to Alaska.

The Majority of Illegal Immigrants Are from Mexico

More than 50 percent of the illegal immigrants in the United States are from Mexico. The second highest percentage is from other Latin American countries, but many of these aliens come through Mexico and cross into the United States. Europe and Canada combined make up only 6 percent of the illegal population.

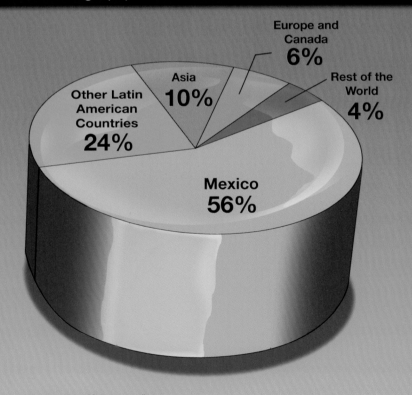

note: figures add to 102 due to rounding.

Source: Hans P. Johnson, "Illegal Immigration," Public Policy Institute of California, 2005. www.ppic.org.

- Between 1993 and 2004, there were an estimated **2,640 deaths** related to border crossing at the U.S.-Mexico border. This is **10 times** the number of deaths reported in Berlin Wall crossings during its 28-year existence.

- In 2003, Mexicans accounted for **91 percent** of all illegal immigrant apprehensions in the United States.

Americans Oppose Driver's Licenses for Illegal Aliens

Rasmussen Reports, a firm specializing in the collection, publication, and distribution of public opinion polling information, reports that a November 2007 poll indicated that an overwhelming majority of Americans oppose driver's licenses for illegal immigrants.

QUESTION: Do you think illegal aliens should be able to get a driver's license?

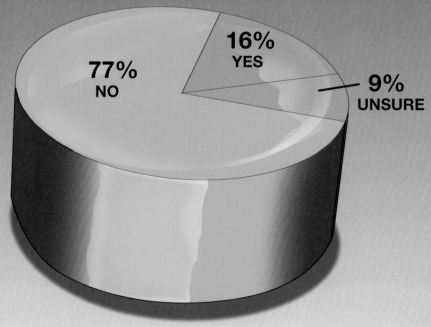

note: figures add to 102 due to rounding.

Source: Rasmussen Reports, November 2007. www.rasmussenreports.com.

Polls Show Increasing Concern over Immigration

A recent survey indicates that over the last several years Americans are growing more concerned that illegal immigrants take jobs and housing from citizens.

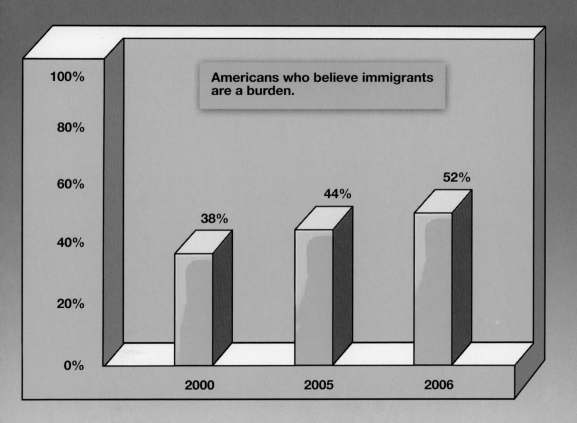

Americans who believe immigrants are a burden.

Source: "America's Immigration Quandry," The Pew Research Center, March 30, 2006. http://people-press.org.

- **Forty-six percent** of illegal immigrants to the United States are women and children.

Does Increased Border Security Protect the United States?

66 We haven't secured our borders, our ports, our mass transit systems. You can go across this country and see so much that has not been done. The resources haven't gotten to the front lines where decisions are made in local government the way that they need to. 99

—Senator Hillary Rodham Clinton, "South Carolina 2007 Democratic Primary Debate."

66 Most Americans will call for more secure borders regardless if accomplishing that means more cops, more jails, more surveillance of all individuals, legal and illegal, crossing US borders, and more money. 99

—Jim Bencivenga, "Is All Well with the U.S. Border Patrol?"

Homeland security is an important issue facing the United States when it comes to border control. If border security is weak, then those who may wish to harm the United States and its citizens have greater opportunities to do so. Particularly since the attacks on the World Trade Center and the Pentagon on September 11, 2001, border security is a major concern for the U.S. government. In the 21st century, terrorism is very much at the forefront of Border Patrol's mission. In fact, according to U.S. Customs and Border Protection:

> In the wake of the terrorist attacks on September 11, 2001, the Border Patrol has experienced a tremendous change in its mission. With the formation of a new par-

ent agency, U.S. Customs and Border Protection (CBP), the Border Patrol has as its priority mission preventing terrorists and terrorist weapons from entering the United States. The Border Patrol will continue to advance its traditional mission by preventing illegal aliens, smugglers, narcotics, and other contraband from entering the United States as these measures directly impact the safety and security of the United States.[12]

Vast Borders and Numerous Points of Entry

There are 326 official points of entry into the United States, and while some of these ports of entry lie along land borders, many more are along coastal areas, waterways, and international airports. According to a report by U.S. Customs and Border Protection:

> On a typical day, more than 1.1 million passengers and pedestrians, including over 630,000 aliens, over 235,000 air passengers, over 333,000 privately owned vehicles, and over 79,000 shipments of goods are processed at the nation's borders. Each represents a potential risk to national security. To protect America from harm, [Customs and Border Protection] must detect and remove the people and goods that pose a threat from the legitimate annual flow of over 400 million people, 20 million cargo containers, and 130 million conveyances.[13]

Particularly since the attacks on the World Trade Center and the Pentagon on September 11, 2001, border security is a major concern for the U.S. government.

These numbers undoubtedly represent a daunting task when it comes to homeland security.

Terrorists Plots

Tensions are high when it comes to border security. There is a real concern that the porous borders could make it easier for terrorists to enter the

United States. The White House has expressed concern that would-be terrorists might see struggles to control the borders as an opportunity for easy access. So far, however, no conclusive evidence exists of specific terrorist plots involving illegal entry to the United States. In fact, organizations such as Annenberg Political Fact Check point out that, while it may be true that easy immigration across porous borders provides a point of entry for would-be terrorists, it is important to remember that all of the 9/11 terrorists were in the United States legally. According to the 9/11 Commission, all of the terrorists on September 11 had visas issued by the U.S. State Department.

> " So far, however, no conclusive evidence exists of specific terrorist plots involving illegal entry to the United States. "

Others continue to point to the opportunities for terrorist plots presented by weak border control. Colin Hanna, founder of the nonprofit organization Let Freedom Ring, a conservative grassroots organization, asserts, "Numerous terrorism experts conclude that the most likely place for a terrorist to enter the United States, even with a suitcase bomb, is the Southwest border."[14] According to Representative Tom Tancredo, the U.S. Border Patrol did report that 946 people from nations of "special interest," Afghanistan, Indonesia, Iran, Lebanon, Pakistan, Sudan, and Syria, were caught attempting to enter the country illegally between 2001 and 2004. Complicating matters, however, is the fact that only 320 of these people from nations of "special interest" were captured at the U.S.-Mexican border. A total of 472 were apprehended at the U.S.-Canadian border, and the rest were caught in Miami, New Orleans, and Puerto Rico ports of entry. These numbers reflect how difficult it can be for a nation with so many entry points to protect its homeland.

Border Security and Crime

In addition to terrorism concerns, crime among illegal immigrants is a growing concern for border security officials. American citizens living in border communities are concerned that illegal immigrants might bring a higher rate of crime because enforcing laws is difficult when a high number of people in these communities are not citizens and can cross back into another country. Recent statistics indicate that there is indeed cause for concern. According to the Federation for American Immigration Reform:

> Criminal aliens—non-citizens who commit crimes—are a growing threat to public safety and national security. . . . In 1980, our federal and state prisons housed fewer than 9,000 criminal aliens. By the end of 1999, these same prisons housed over 68,000 criminal aliens. Today, criminal aliens account for over 29 percent of prisoners in Federal Bureau of Prisons facilities and a higher share of all federal prison inmates. These prisoners represent the fastest growing segment of the federal prison population.[15]

Arizona has experienced a significant increase in property-theft crime in recent years, and many, including government officials like U.S. Representative J.D. Hayworth, attribute this increase to illegal immigration and poor border security. According to Hayworth: "Since 1994 Arizona has led the nation in per capita car thefts, thanks to illegal immigration. In 2002, 57,668 vehicles were stolen in Arizona, mostly by smugglers. Largely because of property theft by illegals, Arizona has the highest crime rate in the nation."[16]

And property theft is just one security issue. According to a 2007 report from CNN commentator Glenn Beck, more than 70 Americans have been kidnapped and killed in the last two years in Laredo, Texas, and the local sheriff links these events to illegal immigrants coming into and out of his community. According to the Laredo sheriff, there is a great deal of lawlessness and gang violence in the border community on the other side of the U.S.-Mexican border in a Mexican town called Nuevo Laredo. According to the sheriff, this gang violence has spread into his Texas community, and he feels powerless to stop it. In a November 9, 2007, program, Glenn Beck reported on the issue:

> A few minutes later I had some people who had family members kidnapped. 70, 70 Americans have been kidnapped and killed in the last two years. That's more than the Iranians took in 1979. And yet we've made calls to

family member after family member after family member. Most of them won't come on television because they will say to you— they will cry on the phone and say, "I can't, I've got other children, I've got to protect the rest of my family, I can't leave here. You don't know what it's like here." These are Americans in an American city.[17]

> **The Immigration Policy Center points out that, while the number of illegal immigrants in the United States has increased significantly in recent years, violent crime rates have declined.**

While such crime rates in border towns like Laredo, Texas, are tragic, the vast majority of illegal immigrants are not criminals and enter the United States for economic reasons, not criminal reasons. Additionally, a 2007 study released by the Immigration Policy Center reports that illegal immigrants do not increase crime. The Immigration Policy Center points out that, while the number of illegal immigrants in the United States has increased significantly in recent years, violent crime rates have declined. However, while national crime rates may be down, there are undoubtedly problems in border communities. In fact, the U.S. Department of Justice reports particular criminal problems in Arizona, especially those related to drug trafficking across the U.S.-Mexican border.

Benefits of Increased Border Security

In light of these border security issues, in the last decade more time, energy, and money have been put into border security than ever before. For example, the amount budgeted for border security has increased significantly every year, and President George W. Bush has even requested emergency additional funding for border security. In 2007 nondefense homeland security (which includes funds for agencies like Customs and Border Protection) saw a $2.3 billion increase when compared to 2006. In 2006 Bush presented Congress with a $1.948 billion request for emergency funding for border security. Stricter laws have also continuously been passed. In 2004, for example, Congress passed a law giving Border Patrol agents more power to deport illegal immigrants, citing concerns about terrorists entering the United States across the Mexican and Canadian land borders. Additionally, in 2007 Congress also passed a new law requiring travelers to have passports to travel between the United States and Canada and the United States and Mexico, something that could be done in the past without an official passport. According to Department of Homeland Security Secretary Michael Chertoff:

> Secure documents are a national imperative that will prevent dangerous people from entering our country using fraudulent identification. This initiative fixes a vulnerability first identified by the 9/11 Commission and later addressed by Congress. It will enhance our ability to assess threats and confirm identity at ports of entry, while continuing to facilitate lawful travel and commerce.[18]

The White House reports that the increase in spending on technology and manpower along U.S. borders has produced some positive results. For example, the number of people apprehended trying to cross the border illegally at the U.S.-Mexican border was down 27 percent in 2007 from 2006. Also, as border security spending increased between 2001 and 2006, U.S. border agents apprehended and sent home more than 350,000 illegal aliens with criminal records. The White House also points out that evidence of the success in increasing border security can be found in the fact that the United States has experienced no major terrorist attacks since September 11, 2001. For the time being, the U.S. government has focused on increasing border security by increasing funding for both technology and manpower, though many still worry that although more is being done, it is just not enough.

> " **The White House reports that the increase in spending on technology and manpower along U.S. borders has produced some positive results.** "

Does Increased Border Security Protect the United States?

> ❝The misperception that immigrants, especially illegal immigrants, are responsible for higher crime rates is deeply rooted in American public opinion and is sustained by media anecdotes and popular myth. This perception is not supported empirically.❞

—Ruben G. Rumbaut, in Eunice Moscoso, "Study: Immigrants Do Not Increase Crime," Cox Newspapers, February 27, 2007. www.coxwashington.com.

Rumbaut is a sociology professor at the University of California at Irvine.

> ❝I think when someone comes in this country illegally, it starts a tradition or culture. You come in illegally; everything you do from that point on is illegal.❞

—Gary Rutledge, "Turmoil in Tulsa: The Illegal Immigration Wreck," MSNBC, July 17, 2007. www.msnbc.com.

Rutledge is a political science professor who lives in Tulsa, Oklahoma. He began to speak out against illegal immigration after an auto accident with an illegal immigrant.

Bracketed quotes indicate conflicting positions.

* Editor's Note: While the definition of a primary source can be narrowly or broadly defined, for the purposes of Compact Research, a primary source consists of: 1) results of original research presented by an organization or researcher; 2) eyewitness accounts of events, personal experience, or work experience; 3) first-person editorials offering pundits' opinions; 4) government officials presenting political plans and/or policies; 5) representatives of organizations presenting testimony or policy.

66 Our intelligence agents will tell you that there has been no evidence of any serious attempt of terrorists to come into the United States through the southern border. 99

—Jim Kolbe, in Claudine LoMonaco, "Border Security: Line Blurs on Terrorism," *Tucson Citizen*, September 11, 2006. www.tucsoncitizen.com.

Kolbe is a U.S. Representative from Arizona.

66 When our government fails to enforce immigration law, it sends a signal that our laws don't matter. And when people learn that we won't enforce some laws, they don't respect other laws. The failure to control our borders has lead to a dramatic increase in violent crime in our country. 99

—American Solutions, "Immigration and Border Security," 2007. www.americansolutions.com.

American Solutions is a nonpartisan organization led by former Republican senator Newt Gingrich. The organization seeks to reform public policy by moving past political differences for changes in the United States.

66 Illegal migration undermines our national security. 99

—Michael Chertoff, "Ask the White House," The White House, September 11, 2006. www.whitehouse.gov.

Chertoff has served under President George W. Bush as the secretary of the Department of Homeland Security since 2005.

❝In the face of mounting terrorist threats and the documented apprehension of terrorists entering the United States across the Canadian border, current border staffing shortfalls expose our nation to an unacceptable risk of security lapses.❞

—Gary Locke, "Governor Gary Locke," State of Washington, December 5, 2001. www.digitalarchives.wa.gov.

Locke served two terms as governor for the State of Washington from 1996 to 2005.

....

❝A vulnerable border also gives terrorists opportunities to smuggle weapons of mass destruction into the U.S. undetected.❞

—Rick Perry, "Border Security Plans for Texas," Office of the Governor, 2007. www.governor.state.tx.us.

Perry has been governor of Texas since 2000, when George W. Bush left the office to become president of the United States.

....

❝Read al-Qaida's training manual. Their modus operandi has been to use the existing systems, to come in legally so people won't notice you.❞

—Margaret Stock, in Claudine LoMonaco, "Border Security: Line Blurs on Terrorism," *Tucson Citizen*, September 11, 2006. www.tucsoncitizen.com.

Stock is a professor of national security and immigration law at the U.S. Military Academy at West Point.

....

❝I think we have a great plan in mind as we step into the future for port security and our challenge is to rise together in the industry locales and to the policy areas in Washington to accomplish what we have set out to do.❞

—James Loy, "Ask the White House," The White House, March 2, 2004. www.whitehouse.gov.

Loy has been the deputy secretary of the U.S. Department of Homeland Security since 2003.

....

❝We have never had a credible plan to enforce the southern border.❞

—Michael P. Jackson, "Government Computer News," GCN, November 12, 2007. www.gcn.com.

Jackson has been the deputy secretary of the U.S. Department of Homeland Security since 2005.

....

❝Our borders are much too porous. . . . We want to keep them open, but we also have to be much more careful. . . . Right now, if you get on an airplane [to the United States] and claim asylum . . . when you arrive at Kennedy Airport in New York, they will say to you, 'OK, we'll give you a hearing on whether you deserve asylum. Show up in a year.' And two-thirds of the people never show up.❞

—Charles E. Schumer, "CBS: Face the Nation," March 7, 1993.

Schumer is a senior U.S. Senator from the state of New York.

....

66 The wacky world of immigration reform is full of half-baked ideas, but none has the taste of having spent less time in the oven than letting local cops enforce federal immigration law. **99**

—Ruben Navarrette Jr., "Commentary: Local Police Shouldn't Enforce
Immigration Law," CNN.com, October 22, 2007. www.cnn.com.

Navarrette is a member of the editorial board of the *San Diego Union-Tribune* and a nationally syndicated columnist.

Facts and Illustrations

Does Increased Border Security Protect the United States?

- After the terrorist attacks on September 11, 2001, President George W. Bush issued an executive order establishing the **Department of Homeland Security** on October 8, 2001.

- U.S. Customs and Border Protection became a part of the Department of Homeland Security in 2003. Among its other duties, **Customs and Border Protection** works to protect U.S. borders within the realm of homeland security.

- On a typical day, Customs and Border Protection processes **1.1 million passengers and pedestrians** and **85,300 shipments** of goods and makes 63 arrests at ports of entry.

- On a typical day, U.S. Customs and Border Protection agents **rescue eight illegal immigrants** who have attempt to enter the United States border across dangerous terrain.

- U.S. Customs and Border Protection agents have over **400 laws** to enforce.

- In a 2006 survey of federal employees, the federal Office of Human Resources Management reported that out of **36 federal agencies**, people working for the Department of Homeland Security ranked **thirty-sixth** in the job satisfaction index.

Americans Think Police Should Check Citizenship Status

According to a November 2007 poll conducted by Rasmussen Reports, more than 70 percent of Americans want police to check citizenship status of all traffic violators. The majority of people believe this would identify many illegals who would otherwise go unnoticed and appropriate measures could then be taken.

QUESTION: Do you think police officers should check traffic violators' citizenship status?

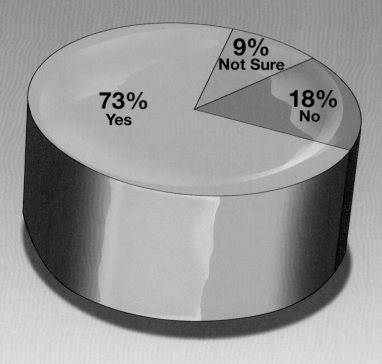

9%
Not Sure

73%
Yes

18%
No

Source: Rasmussen Reports, November 2007. www.rasmussenreports.com.

- Border Patrol agents routinely seize over **1 million pounds (446t) of marijuana** and 15 to 20 tons (13.4 to 17.9t) of cocaine each year.

- Each year, Border Patrol agents arrest hundreds of illegal immigrants from **"special interest"** countries that the federal government considers a potential threat to national security. Since 2001, however, none of those arrested were would-be terrorists.

Impact of Border Patrol Agents

According to the Department of Homeland Security, the federal government plans to significantly increase the number of border patrol agents by 2008. In fact, the number of agents will almost double between 2001 and 2008. The next two graphs show a positive correlation between the number of border patrol agents and illegal immigrant aprehensions.

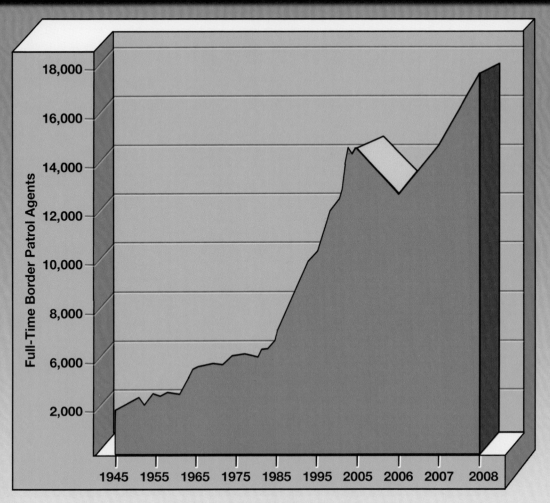

Source: Transactional Records Access Clearinghouse, Syracuse University, 2006. http://trac.syr.edu.

- Since 2001 all Customs and Border Protection port inspectors have been on **Alert Level One**. This means inspectors dramatically enhance inspections of cargo entering the United States.

Recent Apprehension Rates Decline as Security Is Increased

According to the Department of Homeland Security, as border security efforts increased in 2005–2006, the number of apprehensions of illegal immigrants has decreased. Increased border security appears to deter illegal crossings indicating positive results of recent efforts.

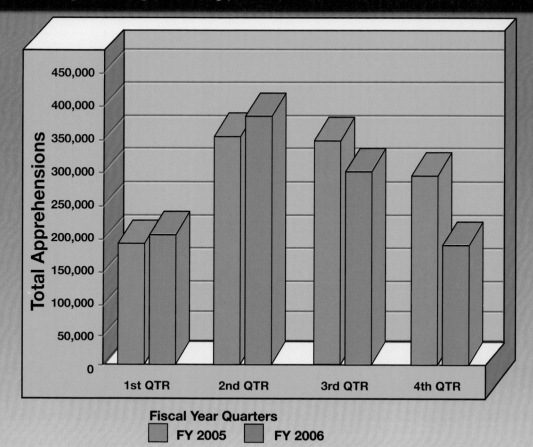

Fiscal Year Quarters
FY 2005   FY 2006

Source: Department of Homeland Security, February 8, 2007. www.dhs.gov.

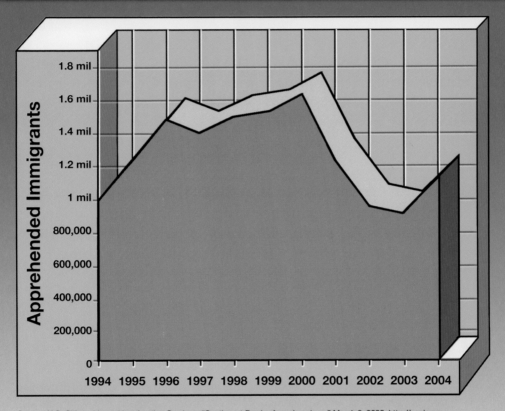

Apprehension of Undocumented Immigrants at Southwest Border

This line graph indicates the number of illegal immigrants apprehended at the U.S.-Mexican border between 1994 and 2004. In 2000, apprehensions peaked at over 1.6 million illegals.

Source: U.S. Citizenship and Immigration Services, "Southwest Border Apprehensions," March 9, 2005. http://uscis.gov.

- Although public opinion polls show that most Americans believe the U.S.-Mexican border presents the most problems when it comes to security, according to Customs and Border Protection, the vast majority of arrests of people from **"special interest"** countries occur at the U.S.-Canadian border.

"We have a mandate from the citizens of the United States who are no longer just demanding better border security, they are now willing to participate in securing the borders themselves."

—Chris Simcox, in David Holthouse, "Arizona Showdown."

"Part of the problem is not that they [Minutemen] are necessarily doing something wrong. It's that they're opening the doors for some extremists or wackos to join the group and to carry out wrong things in their name."

—Robert Deposada, "Minuteman Project Expands to Northern Border."

Although the federal government has continuously increased the budget for border security over the last decade, some Americans remain concerned about border control issues. According to a 2006 *Time* magazine poll, 82 percent of Americans feel that the U.S. government is not doing enough to keep illegals from entering the country. Some Americans, especially those living in border areas, have become so fed up with illegal immigration that they have decided to take matters into their own hands.

Volunteer Border Security

In 2004 a group of citizens who were frustrated with the weak border control in the United States organized into the Minuteman Project, a group of men and women who monitor the land borders in the United States, especially the U.S.-Mexican border, and report illegal immigrants to the authorities. These volunteers were concerned about the impact of illegal immigration on their communities but were also concerned about security. The Minuteman Project's founder, Jim Gilchrist, explains:

> Due to the failure of elected and appointed leaders to enforce the law, Americans face a grave threat to the security, sovereignty, and prosperity of our nation. . . . The truth is that hard-working immigrants are not the only people snaking their way across the border under cover of night. Criminals and terrorists cross the border right along with them.[19]

Although the group is clearly emotionally charged, Gilchrist emphasizes that it is not violent and that its purpose is simply to assist Border Patrol agents. According to Gilchrist and official Minuteman Project guidelines, volunteers should "simply observe and report. Report all suspected illegal crossings, aliens, and activity to the nearest Border Patrol Station or field agent."[20]

In 2006 the Minutemen began another project related to border security; they began a fence-building project in Arizona. A group of volunteers is currently building fences on donated land with millions of dollars of donated money and materials. Since the Minutemen began their own fence, Congress approved funding for federal fencing along the U.S.-Mexican border, something for which Minuteman leader Chris Simco credits the Minuteman Border Fence Project. According to the organization's Web site, "the Feds are building it [the border fence] *because* the Minutemen are building it."[21]

> " According to a 2006 *Time* magazine poll, 82 percent of Americans feel that the U.S. government is not doing enough to keep illegals from entering the country. "

While leaders of the Minuteman Project assert that the group is nonviolent and tout the success of volunteer border patrols as well as the success of the Border Fence Project, the group has been highly controversial.

President George W. Bush has called the Minutemen vigilantes, and reports of racism have surfaced. Many ideas espoused by leaders of the Minuteman Project certainly seem noble. The group claims to want to help peacefully enforce the law and protect American lives and property. And Gilchrist writes in his book *Minutemen: The Battle to Secure America's Borders*, "The Minuteman Project's goals are simple. We want to raise national awareness of the decades-long disregard of the illegal-immigration crisis, and we want to prove that the mere physical presence of watchers can seal the border."[22] Unfortunately, things are not always that simple.

Controversy Surrounds Minuteman Project

The person-hours being donated to border control by the Minuteman Project have been praised by California governor Arnold Schwarzenegger, but the American Civil Liberties Union (ACLU) has voiced concerns about human rights violations. While some praise the group's efforts to assist the U.S. government in border patrol, others are concerned that since the volunteers do not work for the government it can be difficult to monitor activity and make sure group members are not breaking laws or violating human rights.

> The person-hours being donated to border control by the Minuteman Project have been praised by California governor Arnold Schwarzenegger, but the American Civil Liberties Union (ACLU) has voiced concerns about human rights violations.

According to a 2006 report by David Holthouse of the Southern Poverty Law Center, not all is as it seems with the Minuteman Project. Jim Gilchrist, the group's leader, told reporters: "We are not racists. We don't endorse racism, and we're not a hate group. We've told white supremacists they're not welcome here, and we've kept them out. . . . We are not in favor of violence, and we don't hate immigrants." But according to Holthouse, as soon as Gilchrist left the area, two Minuteman volunteers contradicted Gilchrist's claims. One Minuteman volunteer reportedly said, "It should be legal to kill illegals. Just shoot 'em on sight. That's my immigration policy recommendation. You break into my country, you die."[23] Many Minutemen do carry weapons as they volunteer along the border.

Perhaps the biggest controversy surrounding this organization is whether or not the Minutemen are vigilantes. In 2005 President George W. Bush called the Minutemen vigilantes, saying, "I am against vigilantes in the United States. I'm for enforcing the law in a rational way."[24] Many agree with the president and worry that even if Minutemen leaders say the organization is peaceful, they cannot control all of their volunteers, and placing people who are often quite angry about illegal immigration on the border with weapons is just asking for a violent incident. Indeed, in 2005, on the tenth day of the official start of the Minuteman Project in Arizona, a man named Patrick Haab was arrested for holding seven undocumented immigrants at gunpoint. Haab was not an official Minuteman volunteer, but he was later heralded by members of the organization. Charges against Haab were later dropped, and organizations like the ACLU worry that this sends the wrong message to people like the Minutemen who volunteer to help enforce the laws without proper training. About the incident, Ray Ybarra, a leader of ACLU observations of Minutemen volunteers, said: "The Minuteman Project spread the message that it's a good thing to wear a gun when you're dealing with migrants. The Patrick Haab case spread the message that it's okay to actually point those guns at people. And I think a lot of vigilantes are just waiting for the signal that it's okay to go ahead and start pulling triggers."[25] Minuteman leaders, however, argue that President George W. Bush, the ACLU, and most of the media are spreading misinformation about the group.

Whether Minutemen volunteers would harm illegal immigrants remains a cause for concern, but many argue that there are other reasons to be concerned about the group, mainly about the message they send to the world about Americans. Richard Hodges, a resident of Cochise, Arizona, where the Minuteman Project began in 2005, had this to say about the Minutemen:

> Some of them seem all right, and I do give them credit for putting their money where their mouth is and for bringing a lot of attention to the problem of illegal immigration. But a lot of them are a little too extreme, a little too racist for my taste. They were talking to me like they're white supremacists or something, and they were assuming I must

be too just because I live here and have to deal with all the illegals. But I don't care too much for those kinds of attitudes.[26]

Hodges represents many Americans who do not have extreme views about the issue and are able to see both sides of the problem with border security along the U.S.-Mexican border. Critics of the Minuteman Project point out that the group assumes too much about average Americans being outraged about porous borders. While national polls indicate that Americans are indeed concerned, polls also show that Americans are divided about how best to deal with the problem. Many Americans do not support the message the Minutemen are sending. Ray Ybarra of the ACLU agrees that the Minuteman Project sends the wrong kind of message about Americans. In a 2005 interview about his experiences observing the Minutemen along the Arizona border, he related the following story:

> **While national polls indicate that Americans are indeed concerned, polls also show that Americans are divided about how best to deal with the problem.**

The defining moment for me occurred on April 10. It was a Sunday night, about 11 o'clock, and my team of legal observers came upon two migrants sitting on the side of the road, surrounded by a group of about five to seven Minuteman vigilantes, who were celebrating while they waited for Border Patrol to show up. As usual, my team got between the vigilantes and the migrants, and we started asking questions.

The migrants said they had been walking for four days, the last day without food or water, and they were in bad shape. It was freezing cold that night. I had on two big jackets, and they only had windbreakers, and they were so out of it that they couldn't even put together complete sentences. To see that sort of suffering and misery right in front of my face was horrible enough, but 10 feet away there was a group of my fellow Americans, and instead of offering these two men a drink of water, or an extra jacket, or even a candy bar, they were celebrating like a bunch of fishermen who just caught a big one. I think that was probably my saddest moment as a U.S. citizen. I was ashamed of my countrymen.[27]

How Effective Is the Minuteman Project?

The Minuteman Project proclaims success on various levels. When the project first began patrolling portions of the border between Arizona and Mexico in April 2005, the group claimed success in deterring illegal border crossings during that month. Even California governor Arnold Schwarzenegger stated in 2005 that the group has "cut down the crossing of illegal immigrants by a huge percentage."[28] However, real numbers are impossible to produce, and many argue that the group's patrolling efforts just move illegal immigrant crossings to other areas. Although Border Patrol agents working near Minuteman volunteers have reportedly been appreciative of the volunteer efforts, government documents indicate that the U.S. Border Patrol tips off the Mexican government to the location of Minuteman volunteers. The Mexican government, in turn, makes this information public and works to inform potential border crossers. The Minuteman Project reports and the U.S. Border Patrol confirms that the number of arrests of illegal immigrants declined along the parts of the border being monitored by Minutemen. However, the reality is that since most potential border crossers would have been aware of the presence of the Minutemen, they would have simply avoided those regions of the border. In fact, reports from the border indicate that since the Minutemen were only able to cover a 2- to 3-mile (3.2 to 4.8km) portion of the Arizona border, illegal immigrants just crossed the border in other areas.

> " However, the reality is that since most potential border crossers would have been aware of the presence of the Minutemen, they would have simply avoided those regions of the border. "

Others simply waited in border towns in Mexico for the heaviest volunteer activity to decrease after the first month in April 2005.

One type of success that seems much more difficult to deny the Minuteman Project is the enormous amount of media and political attention the organization has brought to the issue of border security. It was after the Minuteman Border Fence Project began that Congress approved funding for a federal border fence in 2006. Additionally, the project has received an inordinate amount of attention in the media, and according to group founders, this was a main goal for the group. Minuteman president Chris Simcox says the group's goal was to bring more public attention to the nation's porous borders. However, even this issue is not without a lot of controversy. Some argue that the group is playing upon racial tensions and terrorism fears since September 11 simply for the media attention. According to David Spencer, a sociologist at Trinity Univeristy in San Antonio, Texas, the Minuteman Project plays on "long-standing anti-immigrant sentiments and concerns about national security to get disproportionate media coverage."[29]

It seems that, as a volunteer border security organization, the Minuteman Project has at least been successful in attracting attention to border control issues. While group leaders claim even larger successes, such claims are difficult to validate. It is unknown whether the Minutemen are really a deterrent to illegal border crossings as they claim to be or if people, aware of their presence, are just crossing the border in different areas. Nonetheless, although the organization is extremely controversial, it seems to be gaining members and will continue to be a presence in the United States when it comes to border control issues. The group reflects a reality in the United States that while the federal government has increased efforts to secure the borders, many Americans feel that it is simply not doing enough to stop illegal immigration and protect the United States from drug trafficking and possible terrorist threats.

Primary Source Quotes*

Are Minuteman Volunteers Really Vigilantes?

66 Like their Revolutionary War predecessors who defended America against a hostile foreign power, today's Minutemen have risen up to answer their nation's call against another invasion. 99

—Jim Gilchrist and Jerome R. Corsi, *Minutemen: The Battle to Secure America's Borders*, 2006.

Gilchrist is the founder of the Minuteman Project, a group of volunteers working to prevent illegal immigration at the U.S. borders. Corsi is an author and conservative activist.

66 Because that's [vigilantes] exactly what they are. By their own definition, they're taking the law into their own hands. 99

—Ray Ybarra, "The Watcher," Southern Law Poverty Center, 2005. www.SPLCenter.org.

Ybarra works for the American Civil Liberties Union to monitor Minutemen activity along the U.S.-Mexican border.

Bracketed quotes indicate conflicting positions.

* Editor's Note: While the definition of a primary source can be narrowly or broadly defined, for the purposes of Compact Research, a primary source consists of: 1) results of original research presented by an organization or researcher; 2) eyewitness accounts of events, personal experience, or work experience; 3) first-person editorials offering pundits' opinions; 4) government officials presenting political plans and/or policies; 5) representatives of organizations presenting testimony or policy.

66 I am proud of what the Minuteman Project has done. Not only peacefully volunteered their services to help solve one of our Nation's biggest problems, they have made more Americans aware of the need for stricter enforcement of illegal immigration. **99**

—John J. Duncan, "Congressman John J. Duncan Jr.," U.S. House of Representatives, June 6, 2005. www.house.gov.

Duncan is a member of the U.S. House of Representatives from Tennessee's Second District.

66 We see the Minutemen as an extremist group that espouses hate and vigilanteism and some violence. **99**

—Janet Marguia, in Maria Sudekum Fisher, "'Minuteman' Grandmother Draws Criticism," *Washington Post*, September 20, 2007. www.washingtonpost.com.

Marguia is the president of the National Council of La Raza, an organization focused on reducing discrimination against and improving rights for Hispanic Americans.

66 Those that hire cheap illegal labor skip out on the tax revenue they are supposed to supply, and they deny their workers the benefits they deserve. Frankly, the practice is un-American. **99**

—Frances Fragos Townsend, "Speech at Woodrow Wilson International Center for Scholars," Woodrow Wilson International Center for Scholars, May 17, 2006. www.wilsoncenter.org.

Since 2004 Townsend has been the assistant to the president for Homeland Security and Counterterrorism.

❝So long as there are jobs and there is a demand for labor and we are not serious about cracking down on employers who hire undocumented workers, people will seek to come in.❞

—Maria Echaveste, "Border Security or Boondoggle?" SFGate, February 26, 2006. www.sfgate.com.

Echaveste is an immigration expert at the Center for American Progress.

❝If you are going to build a 12-foot wall, you know what is going to happen? A lot of 13-foot ladders. This is a terrible symbol of America.❞

—Bill Richardson, "Immigration Top Issue at Debate on Spanish-Language TV," CNN.com, September 9, 2007. www.cnn.com.

Richardson is the current governor of New Mexico and was a Democratic candidate for president of the United States in the 2008 election.

❝Fencing, in combination with other things, is useful. One of the things I believe is you have to enforce our nation's borders.❞

—Dianne Feinstein, "Border Security or Boondoggle?" SFGate, February 26, 2006. www.sfgate.com.

Feinstein is a Democratic senator from California serving since 1992.

❝[When it comes to hiring illegal immigrants] honest owners . . . must still compete on an uneven playing field with dishonest owners who break the law with impunity.❞

—David Robinson and Renuka Rayasam, "Will the Immigration Crackdown Work?" CNN Money, September 17, 2007. http://money.cnn.com.

Robinson and Rayasam are writers for *Fortune*, a magazine devoted to issues in business.

❝Illegal aliens in our city create an economic burden that threatens our quality of life.❞

—Lou Barletta, "Federal Court Throws Out Limits on Illegal Immigrants," CNN.com, July 27, 2007. www.cnn.com.

Barletta is the mayor of Hazleton, Pennsylvania.

❝They [American workers] feel that they are losing jobs. They feel like they are losing health care. They feel that they are falling behind, and their children won't have a better future. So a president has to speak out forcefully against anti-immigrant sentiment and racist sentiment, but also has to make sure that all workers are being tended to.❞

—Barack Obama, "Immigration Top Issue at Debate on Spanish-Language TV," CNN.com, September 9, 2007. www.cnn.com.

Obama is the current senator for the state of Illinois and serves on various committees, among these the Senate Committee on Foreign Relations and the Senate Committee on Homeland Security and Governmental Affairs. He is a Democratic candidate for president of the United States in the 2008 election.

"I have said that Mexico does not stop at its border, that wherever there is a Mexican, there is Mexico. And, for this reason, the government action on behalf of our countrymen is guided by principles, for the defense and protection of their rights.**"**

—Felipe Calderon, "Dobbs: Mexican President's Blatant Hypocrisy," CNN.com, September 5, 2007. www.cnn.com.

Calderon has been the president of Mexico since 2006.

Facts and Illustrations

Are Minuteman Volunteers Really Vigilantes?

- Federal statistics indicate that some illegal immigrants are repeat offenders when it comes to crime. In 2005 the U.S. Department of Justice reported that the illegal aliens in state prisons and local jails averaged **eight arrests** per person.

- Although the number of illegal immigrant deaths associated with dangerous border crossing was down from previous years between 2006 and 2007, there were still **400 deaths**, according to U.S. Border Patrol.

- The California Department of Education spends **$2.2 billion** each year on the education of illegal immigrants.

- It is estimated that illegal immigrants pay about **$50 billion** per year in social security taxes, generating between **$6 billion and $7 billion** per year in social security revenue, though they will not be able to access those funds.

- A 2004 report from the Center of Immigration Studies found that illegal immigrants cost the U.S. government **$10 billion** per year.

- In Los Angeles in 2004, **95 percent** of outstanding warrants for homicide targeted illegal immigrants.

- Although illegal immigrants pay a wide variety of taxes, the Center for Immigration Studies reports that they are still a **tax burden** to the U.S. government because of their low wages.

- The U.S. pays **$1.6 billion** each year for illegal aliens in federal prisons.

California Has Highest Number of Illegal Immigrants

This graph shows the 8 states with the biggest population of illegal immigrants. California has the highest number of illegal aliens with over 2 million, and North Carolina has the lowest number with more than

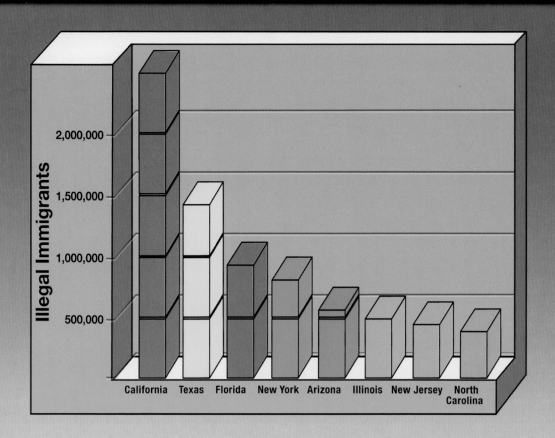

Source: Hans P. Johnson, "Illegal Immigration," Public Policy Institute of California, 2005. www.ppic.org.

- Mexicans living in the United States send more than **$8 billion** per year to Mexico, some say unfairly taking money out of the U.S. economy and putting it into the Mexican economy.

- In the first two months of 208, state lawmakers in the United States proposed a record number of **350 immigration-related bills.** The largest number of proposed laws came from California, Arizona, Rhode Island, Virginia, and South Carolina.

Department of Homeland Security Budget

The budget of the Department of Homeland Security has grown by 49 percent from 2003 to 2008. This increase in budget, in part, reflects an increase in recent efforts to focus more time, attention, and money on border security.

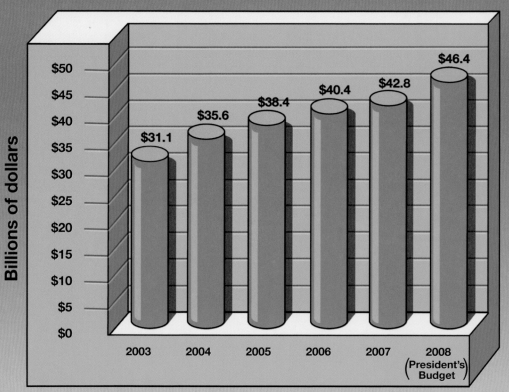

Source: Department of Homeland Security, February 8, 2007. www.dhs.gov.

"La Reconquista" Map Controversial

According to organizations like the Minuteman Project, some radical Mexican organizations plan a "reconquista" or a re-conquest of the southern and western United States. This map (or a similar version) has appeared on several anti-immigrant Web sites and has been published in Minuteman Project publications. The yellow line in the map supposedly indicates the intended Mexican border. While the map is highly controversial as some doubt the authenticity of a plan by immigrants, both legal and illegal, to take over the United States, some radical pro-immigration personalities have referred to parts of the United States as "Mexican states."

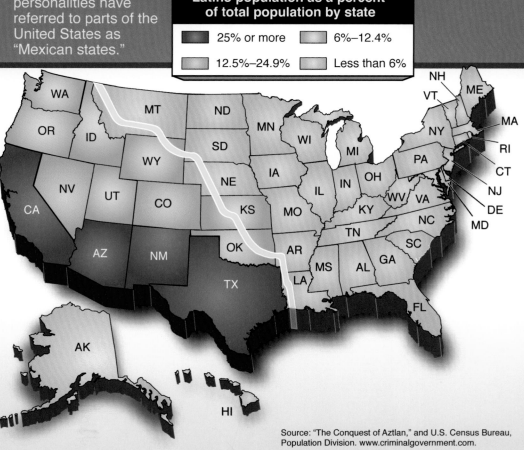

Latino population as a percent of total population by state

- 25% or more
- 12.5%–24.9%
- 6%–12.4%
- Less than 6%

Source: "The Conquest of Aztlan," and U.S. Census Bureau, Population Division. www.criminalgovernment.com.

- In 2007, more than **50 percent** of the illegal immigrants apprehended were caught at the Arizona border.

Immigration Has Small Impact on Size of Workforce

While recent polls indicate that Americans are growing more concerned about the burden immigration places on the United States, the Center for Immigration Studies reports that immigration has relatively little impact on the number of people in the workforce, generally people between the ages of 15 to 64. This chart shows the projected impact of 2 million immigrants coming to the United States each year through 2060. According to this research there would be little difference in the percentage of people in the workforce. This is due largely to the fact that the United States population is already so large.

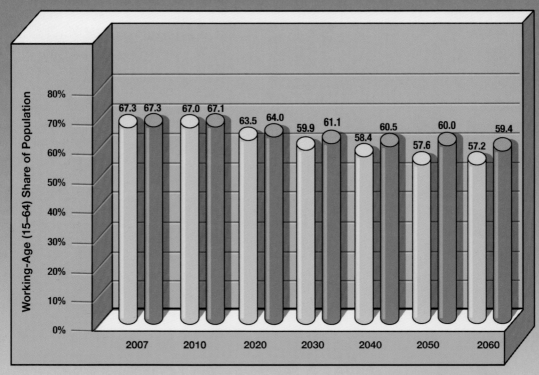

Source: Steven A. Camarota, "One Hundred Million More," Center for Immigration Studies, August 2007. www.cis.org.

Illegal Aliens Have Added Billions to Social Security Fund

According to the Government Accountability Office, billions of dollars have been added to the Social Security fund under Social Security numbers that have been obtained illegally. Illegal immigrants often obtain fake social security numbers, so they can work in the United States.

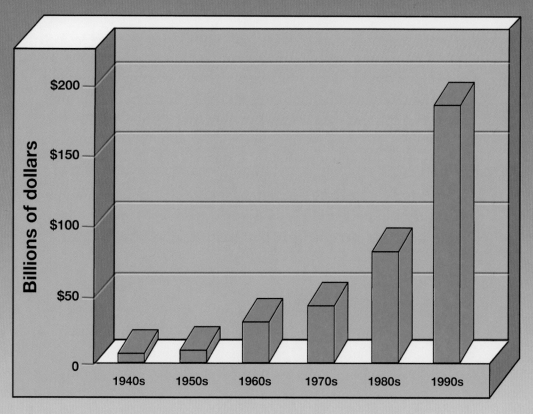

Source: Government Accountability Office, Social Security Administration, from "Illegal Immigrants Are Bolstering Social Security with Billions," Eduardo Porter, *The New York Times*, April 5, 2005. www.nytimes.com.

- According to 2004 research from the Urban Institute, **about 3 million children** of illegal immigrants living in the United States were born in the United States and are, therefore, American citizens.

What Policies Should Guide the Future of U.S. Border Control?

What Policies Should Guide the Future of U.S. Border Control?

❝ Currently, the U.S. seems to be divided on whether to welcome and thank these illegal immigrants (as in the California proposal to allow illegals to get driver's licenses), or greet them at our borders with a shotgun and a glare (as in the 'MinuteMen' vigilante border patrols).❞

—Aaron Krowne, "The Illegal Immigration Problem Is a Tax Problem."

❝ I do have to say that for people who believe the answer is just fence, yesterday we discovered a tunnel. So fencing is not the cure-all for the problem at the border.❞

—Michael Chertoff, "Chertoff: We Can't Really Enforce Laws on Illegals."

As complicated as the problems associated with border security seem to be, with issues related to immigration, terrorism, the economy, and more, solutions to U.S. problems with border control are sometimes even more complicated. As different people assert the effectiveness of their plans, prospects for border security can seem overwhelming at times, and it often seems as if people from each side fail to consider some consequence another side considers most important. For example, those who support fences may not have considered that fences seem to be pushing illegal immigration to other parts of the border or that people have frequently found a way to get past fences. Those who favor fences plus more Border Control agents may not be considering the financial burden that this would present for the U.S. government, which is already in record debt. Economists who argue that economic equality between the United States and Mexico is the only real solution to the problems with the porous borders may have unrealistic ideas about improving another nation's economy.

Enforcing Current Laws

One issue many people raise about border security and immigration is that current U.S. laws are not being stringently followed. Many Americans and formal organizations express frustration that the United States does not enforce current border laws that do, in fact, state that it is illegal to be in the United States without proper documentation. According to U.S. Representative John Boehner, "The American people want our borders secure and our laws enforced."[30] Indeed, the federal government has been working to enforce current border security laws by increasing spending at the border and increasing the number of Border Patrol agents. The White House is currently aiming to increase the number of Border Patrol agents along the U.S.-Mexican border to 20,000 by 2009, for example. Problems with enforcing current laws, however, are many. One of the biggest problems is the money and manpower it would take to actually control all parts of the borders, including extensive land borders with Mexico and Canada and ports. The United States spent about $8 billion in 2007 on border control and protection, and with a national deficit that continues to rise, it is difficult for the government to spend the money it would take to ensure little to no illegal border crossings.

> " The White House is currently aiming to increase the number of Border Patrol agents along the U.S.-Mexican border to 20,000 by 2009. "

More Fences

One of the most frequently proposed solutions to border control problems is to increase the number and size of fences, particularly along the U.S.-Mexican border. In 2006 Congress authorized and President George W.

Bush signed into law the Secure Fence Act. Along with funding for more technology to assist Border Patrol agents, this act provides for hundreds of miles of additional fencing along the U.S.-Mexican border. And in a 2007 "Ask the White House" interview, Secretary of Homeland Security Michael Chertoff said, "One of the things we're insisting upon before anything else happens is the building of the border fence."[31] Essentially, fences are seen as one of the first steps in border security. Duncan Hunter, a Californian Republican member of the House of Representatives, argues that more and better fences are the way to go when it comes to border control. In a 2007 speech he asserted that another 854-foot (260m) fence in California would not only help national security but would also reduce the number of illegal immigrants who are dying in the deserts, crossing the border in dangerous territories. He said, "If 200 kids a year were dying in a canal the first thing you would do is fence it."[32]

> **Many point out that the only way for fences to have any kind of chance at preventing illegal immigration would be to build a fence the entire length of the border. According to the American Immigration Law Foundation, a fence running along the entire U.S.-Mexican border would cost American taxpayers about $9 billion.**

In the last decade, a border fence was built near San Diego, California, and the number of illegal border crossings in that area did decrease significantly. The problem is that the number of illegal border crossings in Arizona rose significantly. But based on the regional success of smaller sections of fences, in October 2006 President George W. Bush signed the Secure Fence Act, which would require the building of 700 miles (1,127km) of fence to be erected in key border locations in California, Arizona, New Mexico, and Texas. Still, many say this is not enough and want to see a fence along the entire 1,952 mile (3,141km) border between the United States and Mexico.

Opponents to more fences claim they are ineffective in general, costly, and more harmful than helpful. According to the American Immigration

Law Foundation, border fencing merely channels undocumented migration to more remote and dangerous terrain. After triple-fencing was constructed in San Diego, apprehensions of undocumented immigrants fell in that area from 450,152 in 1994 to 100,000 in 2002, but apprehensions in the Tucson sector increased 342 percent during this same period. Immigration organizations agree that fences just channel illegal immigration to more dangerous terrain; people desperate to enter the United States have shown that when fences are put up, they will go around them, even if it means risking their lives to cross the U.S.-Mexican border in very dangerous territory. Many point out that the only way for fences to have any kind of chance at preventing illegal immigration would be to build a fence the entire length of the border. According to the American Immigration Law Foundation, a fence running along the entire U.S.-Mexican border would cost American taxpayers about $9 billion. According to an article by Dr. Jason Ackleson published in *Immigration Policy in Focus*, "Building a fence along the entire southwest border would cost roughly $9 billion (about $2.5 billion more than the total budget of U.S. Customs and Border Protection in FY 2005) and is an ineffective means of combating undocumented immigration."[33]

Troop Deployment

In 2006 President George W. Bush ordered 6,000 National Guard troops to the U.S.-Mexican border to help stem the flow of illegal immigrants into the United States. While this move was extremely controversial, according to the Department of Homeland Security, the plan has had some strong signs of success. At the border between Arizona and Mexico where the National Guard troops were deployed, Homeland Security Secretary Michael Chertoff reported that the number of arrests for people crossing the border illegally fell 40 to 50 percent between June 2006 and February 2007. Whether or not these numbers indicate overall success—immigration foundations report that illegal immigrants usually just go around particular regional barriers—the White House sees this small success as an indicator that better border security can be achieved with more guards. The troops at the border were not making arrests but focused instead on aiding Border Patrol agents by watching for illegal immigrants and building vehicle barriers with military vehicles to block portions of the border.

Many people, however, are concerned that such deployment stretches an already overworked National Guard too thin. In 2006 California governor Arnold Schwarzenegger rejected a request from President George W. Bush to send more National Guard troops to the border between California and Mexico. According to Governor Schwarzenegger, more troops at the border would have made it difficult for the National Guard to respond if an emergency happened or a disaster struck.

Quicker Paths to Citizenship and Amnesty Options

One proposed solution that would address the immigration problems with border control if not the security issues would be to provide those who enter the U.S. borders, legally or illegally, with more paths to citizenship. In 2006 President Bush proposed an immigration reform bill that would provide easier access to citizenship for illegal aliens who have been in the United States for more than five years, held jobs, and learned English. These people would be able to pay a fine and have a clear track to citizenship. Others say this is not enough, and many illegals in the country have some support in Congress for different types of amnesty proposals. Although most U.S. political officials seem hesitant to use the word *amnesty*, as the issue is so emotionally charged, congressional leaders like Nancy Pelosi and Harry Reid support amnesty and then fast tracks to citizenship for many of the illegal immigrants living in the United States. Some, such as New Mexico governor and Democratic presidential candidate Bill Richardson, point out that millions of illegals perform jobs and functions essential to the U.S. economy. He questions representations of illegal immigrants as criminals and points out that there should be more representations of the illegal immigrants who clean hotels and bring agriculture to the U.S. economy.

The reality is that the problem of illegal immigrants being an undue burden on social services because they do not pay their share of taxes would be eliminated with programs that would help illegal immigrants become legal and pay the appropriate payroll taxes in addition to taxes like sales tax, which they already pay. Those in favor of this proposal agree that people who come here to work hard and make a better life for themselves and their families should have the same opportunities other immigrants to the United States have had for hundreds of years. Former North Carolina senator and Democratic presidential candidate John Edwards has called for an "absolute path to citizenship"[34] for illegal immigrants as a part of a comprehensive border control plan.

Fast tracks to citizenship are highly controversial, however. Many anti-immigrant and border security organizations oppose granting amnesty to illegal immigrants who have broken U.S. laws by being here without proper documentation. Representative Robert Byrd also argues that amnesty and other fast tracks to citizenship for illegal immigrants already living in the United States are unfair to those who abide by U.S. laws. Byrd has argued: "There are millions of people waiting in line in their home countries to come into the United States legally; those people should not be forced to wait even longer because others have chosen to flaunt the law. Rewarding those who break the laws would serve to encourage more people to rush the borders and break the laws."[35]

> " Fast tracks to citizenship are highly controversial, however. Many anti-immigrant and border security organizations oppose granting amnesty to illegal immigrants who have broken U.S. laws by being here without proper documentation. "

Reduce the Lure of Jobs

Some economists assert that while difficult and complicated, the only truly effective way to deal with border control issues in the United States is to work to establish better economic equality in North America, particularly between the United States and Mexico, and to sanction U.S. employers who hire illegal immigrants. As long as Border Patrol agents are stretched so thin and are so overworked dealing with the millions of people coming to the United States from Mexico for economic opportunity, they will be unable fully to address other issues related to border security, such as would-be terrorists seeking entrance to the United States.

According to Hans Johnson and Mark Baldassare of the Public Policy Institute of California:

> The economic imbalance between the U.S. and other countries will inevitably draw illegal immigrants. Therefore, any successful policy must reduce the allure of jobs. One way is by developing meaningful employer sanctions,

including accurate and verifiable documents that show an individual's right to live and work in the United States. Policies that encourage economic development in immigrants' home countries will reduce the poverty and lack of jobs that pushes so many to migrate in the first place.[36]

Of course, it is important to realize that both economic equality and U.S. employer sanctions are difficult to achieve, though many argue that the latter is at least feasible. Homeland Security Secretary Michael Chertoff has said that employer sanctions are possible if a system to track workers and documents could be established. In the meantime, it is impossible to punish employers who can easily plead ignorant to hiring illegal workers. After all, they have no way of knowing.

Economic development in Mexico is even more problematic. When the North American Free Trade Agreement (NAFTA) was signed into law, Mexico was to be required to develop certain infrastructures, which it did not develop. But who has the power to enforce this law? Certainly, the international community has bigger concerns, such as issues in the Middle East and crises in Africa, so it is difficult for the international community to get involved with the economic situation in Mexico. There are those who think that American companies have the potential to do more for economic development for Mexico. Since NAFTA, companies like Mrs. Baird's, a bread and baked goods company, have moved to Mexico, but many believe they are not doing enough to give back to the communities to which they have moved.

> It is likely that border control will remain an unresolved issue in the United States for years to come.

Although many Americans worry about the effect NAFTA has had on American jobs, as U.S. factories relocated to Mexico for cheaper labor, the reality is that this movement has been hard on the very poor in Mexico as well. Farmers who used to grow food and sell it have been put out of business by U.S. factories. According to one immigrant from Mexico, food that used to take 100 Mexicans to produce can now be produced by 1 Mexican. He said the other 99 Mexicans have no choice but to look for work elsewhere. According to Centolia Maldonado Vasquez: "Before NAFTA, people in rural Mexico were able to survive growing food for themselves and for sale in local markets. Since NAFTA, most people have been unable to compete with imports from the United States and many have been forced to leave their homes in search of dollars."[37]

It is likely that border control will remain an unresolved issue in the United States for years to come. When Irish immigrants came to the United States in large numbers in the nineteenth century, people argued that they were an undue burden on society, and some wanted to send them back to Ireland. And this is just one of many example of America's long struggle with immigration, even though we have often been referred to as a nation of immigrants. On September 11, 2001, terrorism became a new issue for many Americans and one that now complicates border security, which is compounded by massive immigration. There are no easy answers or quick fixes; as border security remains a top priority in the United States, strong leaders will need to work together and think creatively to solve the problems.

What Policies Should Guide the Future of U.S. Border Control?

❝We welcome immigrants, want more of them, and without them this city would not have a future and I believe this country wouldn't have a future.❞

> —Michael Bloomberg, in Alexander Mooney, "Romney Blasts 'Sanctuary Cities' for Attracting Illegal Immigrants," CNN.com, August 21, 2007. www.cnn.com.

Bloomberg is the mayor of New York City, elected in 2001.

❝Immigration laws don't work if they're ignored. That's the problem with cities like Newark, San Francisco and New York City that adopt sanctuary policies. Sanctuary cities become magnets that encourage illegal immigration and undermine secure borders.❞

> —Mitt Romney presidential campaign ad, 2007.

Romney is a former governor of Massachusetts was a 2008 Republican presidential candidate.

Bracketed quotes indicate conflicting positions.

* Editor's Note: While the definition of a primary source can be narrowly or broadly defined, for the purposes of Compact Research, a primary source consists of: 1) results of original research presented by an organization or researcher; 2) eyewitness accounts of events, personal experience, or work experience; 3) first-person editorials offering pundits' opinions; 4) government officials presenting political plans and/or policies; 5) representatives of organizations presenting testimony or policy.

66Overpopulation can be avoided only if borders are secure; otherwise poor and overpopulated nations will export their excess to richer and less populated nations.**99**

—Garrett Hardin, *Living Within Limits*, 1993.

Hardin is an author and a professor emeritus from the University of California.

66We will never regain control of our borders until we have an effective employer sanctions program.**99**

—Romano L. Mazzoli, *Refugee Reports*, September 26, 1994.

Mazzoli is a former Democratic member of the House of Representatives, serving Kentucky's Third District from 1971 to 1995.

66We have the most generous immigration policy, but what is a concern is when illegal immigrants come and undermine a variety of the systems that work in order to make our society function.**99**

—Madeleine Albright, "Albright Says U.S. Doesn't Want to Be Sole Superpower," Associated Press, April 14, 1998.

Albright was the first woman to become U.S. secretary of state in 1997. When she was nominated by then president Bill Clinton and then confirmed by Congress, she became the highest ranking woman in U.S. government history.

66People want to put it all on the undocumented person. They want to believe the negative.**99**

—Larry Dowling, in Oscar Avila, "Priests Speak Out for Illegal Workers," Illinois Coalition for Immigrant and Refugee Rights, March 1, 2006. www.icirr.org.

Dowling is a Chicago-area pastor of St. Denis Catholic Church.

❝Building a fence along the entire southwest border would cost roughly $9 billion (about $2.5 billion more than the total budget of U.S. Customs and Border Protection in FY 2005) and is an ineffective means of combating undocumented immigration.❞

—Jason Ackleson, "Fencing in Failure: Effective Border Control Is Not Achieved by Building More Fences," *Immigration Policy in Focus*, April 2005.

Jason Ackleson is an assistant professor in the department of government at New Mexico State University.

❝Good fences make good neighbors.❞

—Tom Tancredo, "Tancredo Discusses Immigration Reform Bills," Washingtonpost.com, March 30, 2006. www.washingtonpost.com.

Tom Tancredo is a member of the U.S. House of Representatives representing Colorado's sixth district.

❝If people come to the border and figure they can't get in, they'll stop.❞

—Rudy Giuliani, "Giuliani: I Could End Illegal Immigration in Three Years," CNN.com, October 25, 2007. www.cnn.com.

Giuliani was the mayor of New York City from 1994 to 2001 and was mayor when the September 11 terrorist attacks occurred in New York City. He was a Republican presidential candidate in the 2008 election.

66 There is no question that we lack the leadership on the national level to change the tone. And that is the reason why leaders all over the country—mayors and governors—are trying so desperately hard to deal locally with a problem [immigration] that is basically a national problem. 99

—Charles Rangel, "N.Y. Governor Abandons Driver's Licenses for Illegal Immigrants,"
CNN.com, November 14, 2007. www.cnn.com.

Rangel is a Democratic member of the House of Representatives, representing New York's fifteenth District.

66 [Immigration reform is] one of the most complex and emotional issues of our time. 99

—Barbara C. Jordan, Associated Press, October 8, 1994.

Jordan is former Democratic member of the House of Representatives. She was the first black woman from a southern state (Texas) to serve in the House of Representatives. She served from 1973 to 1979.

66 I believe we need to get back to comprehensive immigration reform because no state, no matter how well intentioned, can fill this gap. There needs to be federal action on immigration reform. 99

—Eliot Spitzer, "N.Y. Governor Abandons Driver's Licenses for Illegal Immigrants,"
CNN.com, November 14, 2007. www.cnn.com.

Spitzer was the governor of New York until March 2008, at which time he resigned due to his involvement in a prostitution scandle.

What Policies Should Guide the Future of U.S. Border Control?

- The White House has committed to increasing the number of Border Patrol agents to **18,300** by December 2008.

- By the fall of 2007 the number of U.S. Immigration and Customs Enforcement Teams devoted to removing fugitive aliens had **quintupled** in less than three years.

- Recently, the federal government passed legislation requiring more than **200,000 companies** doing federal business to use **E-Verify**, a system of verifying the status of employees, which will make it more difficult for illegal immigrants to obtain jobs through fraud.

- Under current law, the civil fine for employers who hire illegal workers is between **$275** and **$2,200** per alien for first-time offenders and between **$3,300** and **$11,000** per alien for 4-time offenders.

- In the fall of 2007 the secretary of Homeland Security began delivering regular *State of the Border* reports. These reports keep the American people informed of the federal government's progress in securing the border and hold the administration accountable for continuing improvement.

- Under 2007 legislation the United States plans to build over **370 miles** (595km) of additional fence along the U.S.-Mexican border.

- About **6 million** undocumented immigrants are working in the United States. This represents about **5 percent** of the U.S. labor force.

- Undocumented workers make up about **10 percent** of the **43 million** low-wage workers in the United States.

Work Site Enforcement of Illegals Has Increased

Since 2003, the Department of Homeland Security has improved work site enforcement, working to prosecute unscrupulous employers who hire illegal immigrants. DHS reports an increase in both administrative arrests of people such as managers and corporate officers who hire illegal immigrants as well the number of illegal immigrants who are at work sites during raids and have been charged with criminal violations.

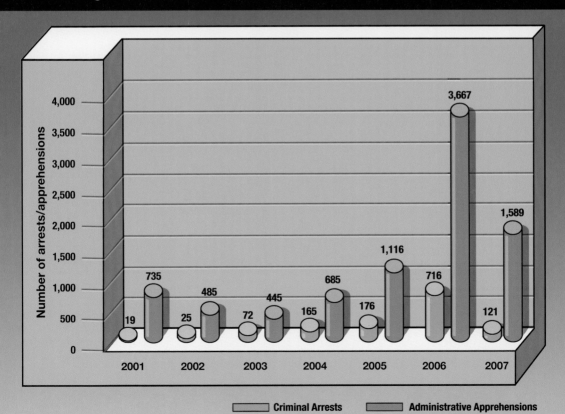

Source: Department of Homeland Security, February 8, 2007. www.dhs.gov.

Secure Fence Act of 2006

This map shows the current fences along the U.S.-Mexico border and the proposed fences that were approved by Congress in 2006. In late 2007 the Border Patrol said that they were only given enough money to build 370 miles of fencing, about half of what Congress originally proposed. Other security measures such as cameras, lighting, and sensors will be added along the fence.

California

Arizona

New Mexico

Texas

Tecate   Calexico

Columbus   El Paso

Douglas

Del Rio

Eagle Pass

Laredo

Mexico

Brownsville

Authorized new fencing

Source: "Senate Backs Mexico Border Fence," BBC News, May 18, 2006. http://news.bbc.co.uk.

- As of 2004 about **3 million** children had been born to illegal immigrants in the United States. These children are U.S. citizens, complicating immigration reform that would require illegal immigrants to return to their country of origin.

- The unemployment rate in the United States has declined, even as the number of illegal immigrants in the United States has increased. In February 2008, the U.S. unemployment rate was **4.8 percent**. In 2003 it was about **6 percent**.

How Americans Want to Reduce Illegal Immigration

According to a 2006 study by the Pew Research Center, nearly 50 percent of Americans say that penalizing employers is the best way to reduce illegal immigration from Mexico. Only 9 percent say that building more fences is the best solution.

What do you feel is the best way to reduce illegal immigration?

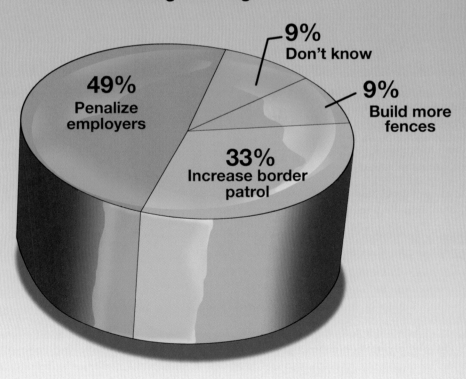

49%
Penalize employers

9%
Don't know

9%
Build more fences

33%
Increase border patrol

Source: The Pew Research Center, "America's Immigration Quandary," March 2006. http://people-press.org.

Key People and Advocacy Groups

The American Immigration Law Foundation (AILF): The AILF was established in 1987 as a nonprofit educational, charitable organization. The foundation is dedicated to increasing public understanding of immigration law and policy and the value of immigration to American society, and to advancing fundamental fairness and due process under the law for immigrants.

Center for Immigration Studies: The Center for Immigration Studies is a nonpartisan, nonprofit research organization founded in 1985. It is the nation's only think tank devoted exclusively to research and policy analysis of the economic, social, demographic, fiscal, and other impacts of immigration on the United States.

Lou Dobbs: Dobbs is a CNN anchor and editor of the program *Lou Dobbs Tonight*. He has been outspoken on issues related to illegal immigration and has criticized the Mexican government's policies.

Federation for American Immigration Reform (FAIR): FAIR is a national, nonprofit, public-interest, membership organization of concerned citizens who believe that U.S. immigration policies must be reformed to serve the national interest.

Jim Gilchrist: Gilchrist is a former newspaper reporter and certified public accountant who started the Minuteman Project. This organization's goal is to help prevent illegal immigration into the United States.

Harvard Immigration Project: The Harvard Immigration Project studies the impact of immigrant students on the American educational system and issues of assimilation as they impact immigrant children.

The Heritage Foundation: Founded in 1973, the Heritage Foundation is a research and educational institute whose mission it is to formulate and promote conservative public policies. Border security and control is one of their primary issues.

The Minuteman Project: The Minuteman Project was founded in 2004 as an organization aimed at preventing illegal immigration in the United States. The group has mainly focused on the U.S.-Mexican border but has recently expanded to address illegal immigration at the U.S.-Canadian border. The organization has been criticized by President George W. Bush but praised by California governor Arnold Schwarzenegger.

Marcelo Suarez-Orozco: Suarez-Orozco is an author, professor, and world-renowned expert on immigration issues. He is a cofounder of the Harvard Immigration Project.

Frosty Woolbridge: Woolbridge is a Colorado columnist who has been outspoken on immigration and border security issues. He writes for the Web site newswithveiws.com.

Chronology

1881–1920
The third big wave of immigrants arrives, mainly from southern and eastern Europe.

1700–1776
The first big wave of immigrants arrives in the U.S. region, mostly from England.

1848
Gold is discovered in California; this results in a wave of Chinese immigration.

1892
Ellis Island, the main entry facility for immigrants entering the United States, opens in New York Harbor.

1790
The U.S. population reaches 4 million.

| 1700 | 1750 | 1800 | 1850 | 1900 |

1820–1870
The second big wave of immigrants arrives, mainly from northern and western Europe.

1846
Millions of Irish migrate to the United States as a result of the potato famine in Ireland.

1886
The Statue of Liberty is unveiled.

1882
The Chinese Exclusion Act is passed.

1900
The U.S. population reaches 76 million.

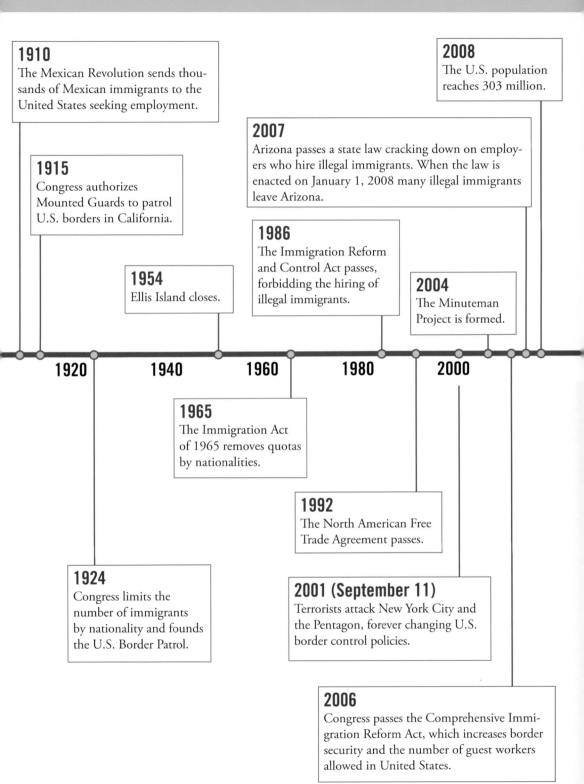

1910
The Mexican Revolution sends thousands of Mexican immigrants to the United States seeking employment.

2008
The U.S. population reaches 303 million.

2007
Arizona passes a state law cracking down on employers who hire illegal immigrants. When the law is enacted on January 1, 2008 many illegal immigrants leave Arizona.

1915
Congress authorizes Mounted Guards to patrol U.S. borders in California.

1986
The Immigration Reform and Control Act passes, forbidding the hiring of illegal immigrants.

1954
Ellis Island closes.

2004
The Minuteman Project is formed.

1920   1940   1960   1980   2000

1965
The Immigration Act of 1965 removes quotas by nationalities.

1992
The North American Free Trade Agreement passes.

1924
Congress limits the number of immigrants by nationality and founds the U.S. Border Patrol.

2001 (September 11)
Terrorists attack New York City and the Pentagon, forever changing U.S. border control policies.

2006
Congress passes the Comprehensive Immigration Reform Act, which increases border security and the number of guest workers allowed in United States.

Related Organizations

American Immigration Control Foundation (AICF)

PO Box 525

Monterey, CA 24465

phone: (540) 468-2022

Web site: www.aicfoundation.com

The AICF is an advocacy group for immigration control. It works to educate leaders and the public about problems AICF believes are caused by illegal immigration. The AICF commissions research on immigration policies.

American Immigration Law Foundation (AILF)

918 F St. NW, 6th Floor

Washington, DC 20004

e-mail: info@alif.org

Web site: www.alif.org

The AILF was established in 1987 as a tax-exempt, not-for-profit, educational, charitable organization. It is dedicated to increasing public understanding of immigration law and policy and the value of immigration to American society, and to advancing fundamental fairness and due process under the law for immigrants. Working closely with leading immigration experts throughout the country, the AILF has established four core program areas: Immigration Policy Center, Legal Action Center, Public Education Programs, and additional activities that include a legal writing competition and immigration awards.

Center for Immigration Studies

1522 K St. NW, Suite 820

Washington, DC 20005

phone: (202) 466-8185

Web site: www.cis.org

The Center for Immigration Studies is a nonpartisan, nonprofit research organization founded in 1985. It is America's only think-tank organization devoted exclusively to research and policy analysis of the economic, social, demographic, fiscal, and other impacts of immigration on the United States.

Federation for American Immigration Reform (FAIR)

1666 Connecticut Ave. NW, Suite 400

Washington, DC 20009

phone: (202) 328-7004

Web site: www.fairus.org

FAIR is a national, nonprofit, public-interest, membership organization of concerned citizens who believe that U.S. immigration policies must be reformed. FAIR was founded in 1979. Its members argue for a temporary moratorium on all immigration except spouses and minor children of U.S. citizens and a limited number of refugees. This moratorium would allow the United States to hold a national debate and devise a comprehensive immigration reform strategy. FAIR would like to reduce immigration numbers to traditional levels of about 300,000 a year.

The Minuteman Project

PO Box 3944

Laguna Hills, CA 92654

phone: (949) 587-5199

Web site: www.minutemanproject.com

The Minuteman Project was founded by Jim Gilchrist in 2004 in response to what the group calls "neglectful" border control and immigration policy enforcement of the U.S. government. Minutemen volunteer at the U.S. borders to help stem the flow of immigration. This group has been highly controversial, receiving criticism from President George W. Bush. However, the organization asserts that it exists to provide assistance to Border Patrol agents and its members do not take the law into their own hands.

National Immigration Forum

50 F St. NW, Suite 300
Washington, DC 20001
phone: (202) 347-0040
fax: (202) 347-0058
Web site: www.immigrationforum.org

The National Immigration Forum is a coalition working to extend and defend the rights and opportunities of immigrants and help the communities where they settle. The National Immigration Forum conducts applied research and policy analysis on immigration topics.

U.S. Border Watch

6046 F.M. 2920, Suite 401
Spring, TX 77379
phone: (800) 759-0948
Web site: www.USborderwatch.com

U.S. Border Watch is a citizens' action group whose focus is to stem the flow of illegal immigration into the United States. It was created to bring media attention to border issues and to fight to get politicians to work harder for border security.

U.S. Citizenship and Immigration Services

425 Eye St. NW
Washington, DC 20536
phone: (202) 514-5231
Web site: http://uscis.gov

U.S. Citizenship and Immigration Services is the federal agency that oversees immigration. Its statistics office keeps records on immigration in the United States.

U.S. Customs and Border Protection

1300 Pennsylvania Ave.

Washington, DC 20229

phone: (202) 354-1000

Web site: www.cbp.gov

The U.S. Customs and Border Protection is the single, unified border agency of the United States. Its mission is to protect the border of America in order to protect the American people. U.S. Customs and Border Protection is responsible for border security, port security, trade inspecting, and several other aspects of American security.

U.S. Department of Homeland Security

Washington, DC 20528

phone: (202) 282-8000

Web site: www.dhs.gov

The Department of Homeland Security is a cabinet department of the U.S. federal government. Established in 2002, the department is responsible for protecting Americans from domestic emergencies, particularly terrorist attacks.

For Further Research

Books

Peter Andreas, *Border Games: Policing the U.S.-Mexico Divide.* Ithica, NY: Cornell University Press, 2001.

Jim Gilchrist and Jerome R. Corsi, *Minutemen: The Battle to Secure America's Borders.* Los Angeles: A World Ahead, 2006.

J.D. Hayworth and Joe Eule, *Whatever It Takes: Illegal Immigration, Border Security, and the War on Terror.* Washington, DC: Regnery, 2006.

David Hunt, *On the Hunt: How to Wake Up Washington and Win the War on Terror.* New York: Crown, 2007.

Heather Mac Donald et al., *Immigration Solution: A Better Plan than Today's.* Chicago: Ivan R. Dee, 2007.

Robert Lee Maril, *Patrolling Chaos: The United States Border Patrol in Deep South Texas.* Lubbock: Texas Tech University Press, 2004.

Paul V. Morris and Christopher C. Bolkcom, *Border Security (or Insecurity).* New York: Nova Science, 2005.

Tony Payan, *The Three U.S.-Mexico Border Wars: Drugs, Immigration, and Homeland Security.* Westport, CT: Praeger Security International, 2006.

Christopher Rudolph, *National Security and Immigration: Policy Development in the United States and Western Europe Since 1945.* Palo Alto, CA: Stanford University Press, 2006.

John Tirman, *The Maze of Fear: Security and Migration After 9/11.* New York: New Press, 2004.

Periodicals

Pedro H. Albuquerque, "When Laredo Turned the Tables on Crime," *Crime and Justice International*, 2006.

Holly Bailey, Daren Briscoe, and Richard Wolffe, "A Border War," *Newsweek*, April 3, 2006.

Marc Bain, "Closing Breaches in Our Borders," *Newsweek*, November 7, 2007.

Michael Barone, "Living with Illegals?" *U.S. News & World Report*, April 3, 2006.

Robert Cliffard, "National Security in the 21st Century," *Military Technology*, 2007.

Commonweal, "Immigration Reform," June 2, 2006.

CQ Weekly, "Immigration," January 2, 2006.

Lou Dobbs, "Our Borderline Security," *U.S. News & World Report*, January 3, 2005.

Economist, "Death in the Desert," August 25, 2007.

Don Feder, "Flawed Immigration 'Reform' Will Permanently Change U.S.," *Human Events*, July 11, 2007.

Katherine Mangan, "Fence and Sensibility," *Chronicle of Higher Education*, July 6, 2007.

Reuben Navarrette Jr., "The Politics of Immigration," *Hispanic*, November 2006.

Anne Plummer, "Shoring Up Border Security," *CQ Weekly*, May 22, 2006.

Romesh Ratnesar et al., "Halting the Next 9/11," *Time*, August 2, 2004.

William Schneider, "The Politics of Illegal Immigration," *National Journal*, June 17, 2006.

Wayne Simmons, "Serious Ideas for Border Security," *Human Events*, June 4, 2007.

Geri Smith, "A Border Transformed," *Business Week*, August 1, 2005.

Paul Starr, "Why Immigration Reform?" *American Prospect*, July/August 2007.

Chris Strohm, "Senate Demands Tighter Security Along Northern Border," *Congress Daily*, September 27, 2007.

Alex Wayne, "Getting Tough on Illegal Immigration," *CQ Weekly*, December 26, 2005.

Internet Sources

Judith Gans, *The Economic Impacts of Immigrants in Arizona.* Udall Center for Studies in Public Policy, University of Arizona. July 2007. www.udallcenter.arizona.edu.

Aaron Krowne, "The Illegal Immigration Problem Is a Tax Problem," Binary Realm Web, December 18, 2007. http://br.endernet. org/~akrowne/writings/illegal_immigration.

Laura Parker, "USA Just Wouldn't Work Without Immigrant Labor," *USA Today*, July 22, 2001. www.usatoday.com.

The Pew Research Center, "America's Immigration Quandary," March 30, 2006. http://people-press.org.

Louis Uchitelle, "NAFTA Should Have Stopped Illegal Immigration, Right?" *New York Times*, February 18, 2007. www.nytimes.com.

Source Notes

Overview

1. Public Agenda, "Immigration: People's Chief Concerns," 2006. www.public agenda.org.
2. Judith Gans, *The Economic Impacts of Immigrants in Arizona.* Udall Center for Studies in Public Policy, University of Arizona. July 2007. www.udall center.arizona.edu.
3. Quoted in Manhattan Institute for Policy Research, "Testimony," April 13, 2005. www.manhattan-institute.org.
4. Quoted in J.D. Hayworth and Joe Eule, *Whatever It Takes: Illegal Immigration, Border Security, and the War on Terror.* Washington, DC: Regnery, 2006, p. 6.
5. Jon E. Dougherty, *Illegals: The Imminent Threat Posed by Our Unsecured U.S.-Mexico Border.* Nashville, TN: WND, 2004, p. 53.
6. Quoted in The White House, "President Bush Proposes New Temporary Worker Program," January 2004. www.whitehouse.gov.

What Are the Impediments to Effective Border Control?

7. U.S. Customs and Border Protection, "Border Patrol Overview," 2006. www. cbp.gov.
8. Laura Parker, "USA Just Wouldn't Work Without Immigrant Labor," *USA Today*, July 22, 2001. www.usa today.com.
9. Quoted in Hoover Institution, "Southern Exposure: Mexican Immigration," *Uncommon Knowledge*, August 26, 2003. www.hoover.org.
10. Quoted in CNN Transcripts, "Many Mexicans Risk Lives in Effort to Cross U.S. Mexican Border and Capture

American Dream," September 2001. www.cnn.com.
11. Quoted in Faye Bowers, "Employers Risk Little in Hiring Illegal Labor," *Christian Science Monitor*, April 18, 2006. www.csmonitor.com.

Does Increased Border Security Protect the United States?

12. U.S. Customs and Border Protection, "CBP Border Security Spotlight," November 7, 2007. www.cbp.gov.
13. U.S. Custom and Border Protection, "Securing America's Borders at Ports of Entry," September 2006. www.cbp. gov.
14. Quoted in FactCheck.org, "We Need a Fence?" October 20, 2005. www. factcheck.org.
15. Federation for American Immigration Reform, "Criminal Aliens," October 2002. www.fairus.org.
16. Quoted in J.D. Hayworth and Joe Eule, *Whatever It Takes: Illegal Immigration, Border Security, and the War on Terror.* Washington, DC: Regnery, 2006, p. 33.
17. Glenn Beck, "Boiling Point," November 9, 2007. www.glennbeck.com.
18. Quoted in Department of Homeland Security, "WHTI Land and Sea Notice of Proposed Rulemaking Published," June 20, 2007. www.dhs.gov.

Are Minuteman Volunteers Really Vigilantes?

19. Jim Gilchrist and Jerome R. Corsi, *Minutemen: The Battle to Secure America's Borders.* Los Angeles: A World Ahead, 2006, p. 4.
20. Gilchrist and Corsi, *Minutemen*, appendix.

21. Minuteman Border Fence, "Welcome to the Minuteman Border Fence." www.minutemanhq.com.

22. Gilchrist and Corsi, *Minutemen*, p. 9.

23. Quoted in David Holthouse, "Arizona Showdown," Southern Poverty Law Center, 2006. www.SPLCenter.org.

24. Quoted in James G. Lakely, "Bush Decries Border Project," *Washington Times*, March 24, 2005. www.washingtontimes.com.

25. Quoted in Mark Potok, "Vigilantes and the Law," Southern Poverty Law Center, 2005. www.SPLCenter.org.

26. Quoted in Holthouse, "Arizona Showdown."

27. Quoted in Southern Poverty Law Center, "The Watcher," 2005. www.SPLCenter.org.

28. Quoted in Carla Marinucci and Mark Martin, "Governor Endorses Minutemen on Border," *San Francisco Chronicle*, April 29, 2005. www.sfgate.com.

29. Quoted in Brady McCombs, "Minuteman Patrols Ready to Return to Arizona Border," *Arizona Daily Star*, March 21, 2006. www.azstarnet.com.

What Policies Should Guide the Future of U.S. Border Control?

30. Quoted in Mark Silva, "Bush Administration: 'Improving Border Security,'"
Chicago Tribune, August 10, 2007. http://weblogs.chicagotribune.com.

31. Michael Chertoff, "Ask the White House," June 7, 2007. www.whitehouse.gov.

32. Quoted in Eunice Moscoso, "Democrats Promise Immigration Reform; No More Fences," Cox News Service, July 1, 2007. www.coxwashington.com.

33. Jason Ackleson, "Fencing in Failure: Effective Border Control Is Not Achieved by Building More Fences," *Immigration Policy In Focus*, executive summary, April 2005.

34. Quoted in Moscoso, "Democrats Promise Immigration Reform; No More Fences."

35. Robert C. Byrd, "Standing for Strong Borders and Against Amnesty," April 2006. http://byrd.senate.gov.

36. Hans Johnson and Mark Baldassare, "Commentary: A Way to Common Ground in California," Public Policy Institute of California, 2007. www.ppic.org.

37. Quoted in "Breaking News from Oregon: OR and Mexico Labor Leaders Rally Against NAFTA Expansion," Eyes on Trade, October 25, 2007. http://citizen.typepad.com.

List of Illustrations

Index

About the Author

Crystal D. McCage holds a PhD in rhetoric from Texas Woman's University. She is an assistant professor of rhetoric and composition at a small, private university in Maine. This is her third book for ReferencePoint Press.